Confronting Church and State
Memoirs of an Activist

John M. Swomley

HUMANIST PRESS

Amherst, New York

For Marjie

Published by Humanist Press in cooperation with Americans for Religious Liberty.

Humanist Press is a division of the American Humanist Association, 7 Harwood Drive/P.O. Box 1188, Amherst, NY 14226-7188, (716) 839-5080.

Americans for Religious Liberty (ARL), P.O. Box 6656, Silver Spring, MD 20916, is a nonprofit public interest educational organization, founded in 1981, dedicated to preserving the American tradition of religious, intellectual, and personal freedom in a pluralistic secular democratic state. Membership is open to all who share that purpose. ARL publishes a newsletter and other material, operates a speakers bureau, and has been involved in litigation in defense of separation of church and state and freedom of conscience. Inquiries are welcomed.

Library of Congress Catalog Card Number: 97-73529

ISBN 0-931779-08-1

Printed in the United States of America

Table of Contents

Forewords

This is an unusual book, in that it has three forewords. One is by one of the country's most prominent Christian leaders, Dr. James M. Dunn, executive director of the Washington-based Baptist Joint Committee on Public Affairs, a major force on the national scene defending religious liberty and the principle of separation of church and state. Dr. Dunn praises *Confronting Church and State's* author as an exemplary Christian activist.

Another is by a Conservative Jewish rabbi, Morris B. Margolies, who lives in Kansas City, as does the author, and has seen and heard the reverberations of the author's work worldwide.

The third is by this writer, a Humanist and Unitarian Universalist who appreciates the author's life and work from a more "ethical naturalist" point of view. John Swomley's life and work, I believe, supports the proposition that there is a core f democratic and ethical values that transcends theological differences, that brings together men and women of disparate traditions, theist and humanist, Christian and Jewish and other, liberal and conservative, in the service of common concerns and in the face of common challenges.

This book is unusual in other ways. It was written after many months of prodding by the staff of Americans for Religious Liberty, who felt the author's national and international activities should be described and chronicled. He is the president of Americans for Religious Liberty, but that is a small and recent part of his long and distinguished career, which includes starting the non-violent movement in the Philippines that resulted in the overthrow of dictator Ferdinand Marcos, and his handling threats of assassination from the far-right "Minutemen" in Kansas City. One of his unique chapters discusses his relationship with William C. Sullivan, Assistant Director of the F.B.I., who sought him out as a confidant during his difficult years under J. Edgar Hoover.

Although this book does not include his memoirs from 1939 to

1960 when he directed the national campaign against universal military training, organized the Committee Against Jim Crow in Universal Military Training and Service which led President Truman to desegregate the armed forces, and was involved in the Martin Luther King civil rights campaign, these are background for his ability to function nationally. For example, he relates all too briefly his quick organization of the American Committee on Korea in 1993 to prevent war between the United States and North Korea and his visits to that forbidden country.

One of the great virtues of this unique book is the way the author was involved in almost every major event or issue in recent history -- the church-state struggles of the 1960s onwards, the aftermath of the Second Vatican Council, the Vietnam War, the Cold War in Europe when he negotiated with an East German official, liberation movements in Latin America, dealing with the far right wing in the headquarters city of the Minutemen, and the continuing struggle against racism and for reproductive freedom for women.

I have had the privilege of knowing and working with the author for many years. His involvements have literally spanned from A to Z, from Argentina to Zimbabwe. He remains an activist in the very best sense of the word and matches the energy of men and women half or a third his age.

I commend this book to the widest possible readership as an example of putting into practice the highest ideals of both religion and ethical naturalism.

-- *Edd Doerr*[1]

John Swomley had made an incredible contribution to peace, justice, compassion and freedom. He is a living rebuke to the conventional wisdom that one individual is helpless. He has been able effectively to cling to the biblical goals without sliding into idealistic irrelevance.

Because he has taken his faith, Jesus' words, the Christian vision so seriously, his life and witness do judge all of us who pay lip

---

[1] President of the American Humanist Association and executive director of Americans for Religious Liberty.

service to a serious ethic but are not always willing to pay the price. His rebuke, however, is not mean-spirited, arrogant or proud. His example is so powerful precisely because it is a happy mix of toughmindedness (he rigorously applies his political science expertise and his keen insights from Christian ethics) and tenderheartedness.

Here is a treasure trove of information and inspiration.

-- James M. Dunn

There are thinkers who *do* not. There are doers who *think* not. John M. Swomley's distinguished career has been marked by both thinking and doing.

Primarily what he has thought is that God represents justice and compassion. Therefore all of his life has been dedicated to the never ending struggle for implementing both. Swomley, the theologian, has regarded our role on earth as instruments of God in the pursuit of equity and decency for all of His creatures.

There is hardly a cause involving the alleviation of human deprivation in which Dr. Swomley has not been involved. He has been a diligent worker in the Lord's vineyard in the face of formidable obstacles. In the process, he has never lost his grace, his dignity and -- above all -- his humanity.

Like all dissenters from the Establishment, he has often been reviled, threatened and calumniated. But he has never cowered and has never wavered. His *Memoirs of an Activist,* which are published herewith, represent only a partial record of the lifework of a most unusual servant of God: one who believes with all his heart that the most effective road to Godliness is the amelioration of suffering on his earth and that the path back to Eden can be negotiated if only we banish the flaming sword of the cherubim from its gates.

-- Morris B. Margolies

Preface

The publisher has insisted on a brief biographical sketch, although this book is not a biography, but is instead a memoir of the struggle for religious liberty in which I have been a part.

All of us are heirs of our past and the culture in which we were reared. I was born in Harrisburg in conservative Central Pennsylvania May 31, 1915, the child of two loving and caring parents, John Montgomery Swomley and Florence Edna Forsyth. Two sisters, Jean Elizabeth and Dorothy Forsyth followed in the next few years, and much later, a brother was born, James, fourteen years younger than I.

While attending excellent public schools, I became interested in public speaking, and in 1932 won the Pennsylvania state high school oratorical contest. Unfortunately, I had no experience in extemporaneous speaking, so placed third in the national semi-finals.

When I graduated the United States was well into the Great Depression, and my parents were unable to finance attendance at college. However, my father was successful in getting me work as a page in the Pennsylvania Senate at a salary of two dollars a day. I enrolled in Dickinson College, twenty miles from the capital, and received permission to take morning classes and work the rest of the day.

After four years at Dickinson, where I won the senior history prize and was elected Phi Beta Kappa, I enrolled in Dickinson Law School. Before the year ended I decided against law and resigned without knowing what I wanted to do. The editor of Harrisburg's newspaper, *The Patriot and Evening News,* who was a frequent visitor and alumnus of the fraternity I had joined, told me I ought to go into "cause work" because I seemed to have strong convictions on issues.

That summer of 1937 I was urged by conservative Methodist pastors to attend meetings of the National Council of Methodist Youth in Evanston, Ill. and try to change it, because they deemed it too radical. Instead, it changed my life. Here were young people running their own meetings, discussing racism, pacifism, and other social issues. I had never had any "Negro" friends, and was

1

assigned a room and shared a bed with James Farmer, who later became a major civil rights leader and a founder of the Congress of Racial Equality (CORE). For the first time in my life I was confronted with the radical dimension of the Christian faith in a group of committed young adults, and forced to rethink everything. By the end of the summer I had made a decision to enroll in the Boston University School of Theology, without any thought of becoming a minister. During my first two years I organized students in small groups to discuss pacifism and other social issues, and persuaded or coerced the Dean, Earl Marlatt, to end discrimination in housing or room assignments. At the annual meeting of the National Council of Methodist Youth, I was elected vice-president.

On a visit to my parents I got into a long and serious argument with my father, who did not agree with my new commitments. My younger brother listened silently. I left the room, certain that there was no point in further argument. A few minutes later when I was about to re-enter the room, I heard my father say, "Now, Jim, you listen to John. He's probably right." He was not prepared to change his long-held beliefs but I never doubted his support.

I inherited from both parents a strong sense of standing up for what is right or just, despite all odds. I was taught to stand alone, no matter what my peers did or the pressure they exerted on me to conform.

While in graduate school in Boston I was invited one evening to attend a meeting of the Greater Boston Student Strike Against War Committee, which planned a student walk-out from colleges to protest preparation for what became World War II. There were about eighty or ninety persons present, evenly divided between communists and their sympathizers on one hand, and socialists and pacifists on the other. They had been unable to agree on a chairperson. When I was introduced as vice-president of the National Council of Methodist Youth, which already had a national reputation against war, I was unanimously elected as their chair. This led me to speak to students in the numerous colleges and universities in Greater Boston and to organize them.

In 1939, after Nazi Germany and the Soviet Union signed a non-aggression agreement, the Communists ceased to be anti-war and left the Student Strike Against War. When plans for the strike nevertheless went forward, some 3,000 students walked out of classes and gathered at the Boston Common. I had in the meantime taught classes in English and parliamentary law to members of the International Ladies Garment Workers Union. It was a great surprise to hear a marching band followed by hundreds of Union members come up Boylston Street to join in the student strike. They were led by Rev. George Paine, a wealthy Episcopalian and Boston "Brahmin" or blueblood, who was a socialist candidate for Governor. He was carrying in a belt holster a huge American flag.

When hundreds of Young Communists tried to break up the demonstration, they were met by numerous mounted police, and we held our strike meeting without further incident.

Also in 1939 I began working part-time as New England Student Secretary of the Fellowship of Reconciliation and organized more than thirty groups in New England, collecting a weekly offering from each. That money, amounting to $40 a month, I sent to the Fellowship in New York to employ James Farmer to work in the Washington, D.C. area.

When I graduated in 1940 I was invited to work for the National Fellowship of Reconciliation. That group readily permitted me to accept a request from the World Peace Commission of the Methodist Church, based in Chicago, to go to Washington to lobby against the draft and for rights for conscientious objectors if it were adopted. I joined two Quakers, Paul Comly French and Raymond Wilson, and the three of us visited members of Congress together. We even met with Eleanor Roosevelt in Hyde Park after conscription was adopted, and received her promise that there would be provision for conscientious objectors in any renewal of the draft.

The story of my war years and postwar peace work is too long to detail here. I did, however, largely direct the national postwar campaign against Universal Military Training. I continued to work for the Fellowship until 1960 when I left to teach social ethics and philosophy at a new Methodist institution in Kansas City, Saint Paul School of Theology. In the meantime I had earned a Ph.D. in political science at the University of Colorado in a year and summer sabbatical in 1957-58.

Introduction

This book concerns action, frequently involving conflict, about religious, political or civil liberty. It begins with defense of religious liberty in the United States, but also involves acts of liberation with respect to Communist rule in East Germany, Argentina under martial law, the Philippines under the Marcos dictatorship, southern Africa under white rule, conflicts with right wing groups and leaders in the United States as well as with other organizations.

Since action flows from some conviction or philosophy, this book also is based on the *concept of liberation* from every form of tyranny, whether religious, racial, economic, political or social custom. It is also based on respect for living human persons and their convictions. Such respect assumes that it is possible to disagree without demonizing another person or seeking to deny another's basic humanity. That therefore means opposing institutions, dogmas, customs, philosophies rather than viewing persons as enemies, even when they identify themselves with such institutions or dogmas. It is frequently possible to share areas of agreement on other issues with those who are adversaries in one area of conflict or disagreement.

However, no one, including this author, can act without failure as well as success. Anyone who defends separation of church and state runs the risk of being at least verbally attacked by those who, for example, want aid to their church schools or other benefits from local, state or national governments. They find it difficult to believe that those who defend separation would defend it even if their own churches and synagogues sought government support.

In my own case I value religious liberty as not only essential to democracy but as the essence of religion itself. Anyone coerced to belong to a specific group or to accept its dogma is not much of an asset to that religious institution. Nominal members are never as helpful as those who are convinced supporters. Beyond that, those who do not feel free constructively to criticize the religion to which they are related, or even other religions, are hardly assets to religion

5

as such. Without helpful, often strong criticism, churches and other religious institutions can become self-satisfied and their own worst enemies.

Religious liberty in the United States has at least four components. One is that no level of government should discriminate for or against people on the basis of their religious profession or lack thereof. This is embodied in Article VI, Section 3 of the Federal Constitution, which forbids any religious tests for public office or for a position of public trust. It also means that persons of a minority religious group or none may not be excluded from public office.

A second component of religious liberty is the idea embodied in the First Amendment that "Congress shall make no law respecting an establishment of religion. . . . " That means that government may not sponsor, support, endorse or finance any or all religious institutions. (An institution of religion is an establishment of religion.) The word *establishment* also has another meaning, because an established church is one sponsored or supported by government. When the First Amendment was adopted, a number of states had what are known as multiple establishments, or government aid to a number of churches. The First Congress wisely decided against support of any or all churches, as well as against designation of a national church. Churches are not only more free to criticize government if it is not their source of income, but also are free to develop their own doctrines and activities without regard to government policy.

A third component of religious liberty is freedom of conscience and the free exercise of one's religion. Freedom of conscience may be exercised contrary to the doctrine of one's denomination of religion, or against the laws or customs of society. People of conscience are rare, but essential to any society. Conscience can require disobedience. In either case, conscientious citizens are the bulwark of any society, church, or nation.

The fourth component of religious liberty is equality of treatment under law. No religious taboo or doctrine against women, ethnic groups, persons of any sexual orientation, persons who choose abortions or perform them, divorced persons, or unmarried sexual partners should prevail in law or in community practice. Religious liberty requires a healthy respect for difference as well as civility in public discourse.

Liberation is not identical with religious liberty, but is related to it. The first step in the direction of liberation is to become conscious of our own vested interests, our own ideological commitments. The second step is to become aware that it is impossible to act or refrain from acting politically without ideological motivation. A third step is to examine ideologies, including our own, critically. Ideology can be defined as an idealized or in some cases absolutized program or philosophy that serves some political or social structure or goal.

There are ideologies that take a part of the human world, such as a race or nation, and idealize its way of life or political program. All ideologies of racial superiority, nationalism, and cultural imperialism are in this category. There are ideologies that take a part of the human experience such as a political or economic system, and idealize it into a way of life, or set it up as a total system through which all of history and reality are interpreted. Capitalism and Communism are illustrations.

There are ideologies that idealize or absolutize a future existence in such a way as to validate the existing order. In this category would fall all those who accept the existing order until God is ready to usher in his kingdom. Some forms of Protestant fundamentalism, in particular, tend to have no concern for changing the social order as such; they tend to view morality as individualistic. They emphasize the sins of sex, but do not concern themselves with the larger sins of militarism, war, capitalism and imperialism which exploit entire populations. Therefore, wrote Peter Berger, by concentrating "attention on those areas of conduct that are irrelevant to the maintenance of the social system," the fundamentalist "diverts attention from those areas where ethical inspection would create tension for the smooth operation of the system. In other words, Protestant fundamentalism is ideologically functional in maintaining the social system. . . . " By the same token, the Catholic hierarchy's concentration on opposition to abortion and contraception diverts attention from the larger problems of poverty and malnutrition caused by military spending, overpopulation, and maldistribution of scarce resources.

Another ideology idealizes or absolutizes an organization or its structures or the pronouncements of its leader as coming from God and therefore not subject to criticism or change. When the leader makes a statement on faith or morals, however timely at the moment, any change in the light of new understanding would reflect on the leadership principle or the leader's perception of revelation. Thus it would undermine the authority of the church or cult. Whenever a church accepts and consecrates human judgments and values, whether a philosophical system or an ancient cosmology or a cultural view of sex or race, or male leadership, it tends to look to the past or have a reactionary bias.

There is of course more to the faith of such churches than ideology. It does, however, indicate that churches are not immune from ideology and succumb to it as well as do political parties.

There is still another form of ideology that idealizes or absolutizes a method of settling disputes or achieving social change. The idea that "power grows out of the barrel of a gun," that revolution has to be violent, that force or violence is the only language that everyone understands, or the outcome of human history is finally determined by war, assumes that ultimate power and hence meaning are bound up with one form of coercion, the ability to intimidate and destroy. Violence becomes the deciding factor in human affairs, not because this is necessarily so, but because it is believed to be so. This ideology, evident in the National Rifle Association, militia organizations, the military-industrial complex and in the identification of patriotism with armed might, is, combined with overpopulation in a world of limited resources, the most serious threat to human survival today.

There are of course other ideologies, but these suffice to suggest that religious diversity and religious liberty can play a major role in human liberation from otherwise uncriticized ideological commitments that threaten the human and environmental future on the planet.

So much of the struggle for religious liberty and for liberation begins within the churches, between those who think of the church as both a wholesome institution for personal nurture of oneself and family, and as a conservative, stabilizing force on the one hand, and those who believe it has a mission to change society and liberate individuals to serve others.

What follows is the account (often surprisingly dramatic), of my efforts to analyze and act on some of the very important religious and civil issues in the United States and abroad.

Chapter 1
Catholicism After Vatican II

The Roman Catholic Church is and has been a very strong presence in American life. Yet as a boy in Harrisburg, Pennsylvania, who attended public school from 1920 to 1932, I cannot remember a single Catholic friend. Perhaps they were segregated in the only Catholic school in our section of the city. I met my first Catholics when I joined a college fraternity in 1932, but there was nothing distinctively different about them from anyone else away from home in the declining years of the Prohibition era. The distinctively different one in our fraternity was myself, a teetotaler.

I am sure there must have been anti-Catholic prejudice in our circles in Harrisburg, from which I commuted to college, but the only actual comment I can remember was a statement of my mother much later. She said, "When you get married, never take your wife to a Catholic hospital."

When I was in graduate school in Boston working part-time in activities to oppose what became World War II, I found a ready reception for my speaking and organizing in virtually every college in New England except Catholic colleges, where there was virtually no student anti-war sentiment.

I did, however, find a kindred spirit in the head of the Catholic Worker House in Boston, a pacifist named Sullivan, who told me that Dorothy Day, the head of the Catholic Worker Movement, had authorized autonomy so that each Catholic Worker House could determine whether to support or oppose the war. Not long thereafter I was invited to participate in a three-cornered debate with Dorothy Day, who espoused the "Just War" position, a rabbi who supported the war, and I, who opposed it on Christian pacifist grounds.

Upon graduation from Boston University School of Theology in 1939 I joined the national staff of the Fellowship of Reconciliation, the pacifist organization founded in 1914 in England and 1915 in the U.S. In 1940, although the country was not yet officially at war, Congress was debating and likely to adopt a bill to conscript all

9

young American men at age 18 for one year of military training, followed by seven more years in the Reserves. This was to be a permanent system after the European pattern. The F.O. R. sent me to Washington to join two Quakers, Paul Comly French and E. Raymond Wilson, in lobbying against conscription and for rights for conscientious objectors in the legislation being debated. Congress did pass the conscription bill, with minimal rights for conscientious objectors.

In 1944, while the war continued, it became obvious that the military would seek permanent postwar military conscription. A group of peace and pacifist organizations began planning for a joint campaign against universal military training (U.M.T.). After its first year of organization I became the director of the National Council Against Conscription. In that capacity I met for the first time important Catholic leaders.

A wealthy Catholic member of the Women's International League for Peace and Freedom, Helene Rea, took me to meet Cardinal Dennis Daugherty, the Roman Catholic Archbishop of Philadelphia, whom I wanted to invite to serve along with four others as honorary chairpersons of the National Council Against Conscription. He agreed to serve, but he wanted regular assurance that we were not involved with Communists.

A second member of the hierarchy with whom I worked was Bishop John Wright of Worcester, Mass. He acted as a representative of Cardinal Richard Cushing of Boston, who was strongly opposed to conscription. Wright later became a Cardinal assigned to Rome.

The two most helpful Catholics at this time, both Jesuits, were Father Alan Farrell and Father Robert Graham, then associated with the Jesuit weekly, *America*.

Since our campaign was prior to the Ecumenical Council and the election of Pope John XXIII, there were no official meetings between Catholic representatives and Protestant, Jewish or other groups. Usually I would propose strategy to a small inner circle and then get separate approval by going to or phoning personnel at the National Catholic Welfare Council, the forerunner to the U.S. Catholic Conference. (The same problem existed between farm and labor groups who would not meet together.) On the whole, the Catholic participation in the campaign was somewhat less than that of the Protestant churches, which in many respects significantly involved their laity.

However, at a crucial point in the U.M.T. campaign, Bishop Wright made an essential contribution. In the weeks before the vote on U.M.T. was to be taken in the House of Representatives, I had paid a pollster to poll all the members of the House so that I knew how each planned to vote. I noted that with one exception the Massachusetts delegation were for U.M.T. I phoned Bishop Wright to ask him if he could change any of these votes. He replied that the Church does not engage in politics and could not influence votes. "In that case," I said, "there is no point in giving you their names." "Oh, yes," he said, "I would like to know who they are." In fact, he changed the votes of all but one.

Over a period from 1944 to 1951 there was concerted, increasing sentiment against installing the European system of universal training, even in a watered-down six-month version the military desperately proposed, and in a dramatic vote in March, 1952, the House of Representatives defeated it. This was in fact the result of the first U.S. cooperative lobbying of peace, church, farm, labor, education, and other groups on a single issue.

In 1953, following the retirement of A.J. Muste, I was asked to serve as the executive secretary of the Fellowship of Reconciliation. After I resigned in 1960 to teach, I was frequently consulted by my successor, Alfred Hassler. One decision on which he asked my judgment was whether the Catholic Pacifist Fellowship should be invited to affiliate with the Fellowship of Reconciliation. I urged him to press forward with the affiliation.

When I went to Kansas City to teach ethics at the Saint Paul School of Theology, I became involved in public hearings at the Missouri Capitol in Jefferson City against various forms of aid to parochial schools. There was a very strong Catholic lobby that promoted such aid. My arguments, however, were never pitched on an anti-Catholic level, but on constitutional and civil liberties grounds. To my astonishment, when I was reported accurately in the Kansas City papers, I received fan mail from professors at Immaculate Conception Seminary in Northwest Missouri. The Seminary was a part of the Benedictine Abbey, and trained young men as parish priests.

At the beginning of the fall term in 1962, I received an invitation from the Dean, Rev. John McCluhan, to speak at Conception. My first talk was to the combined classes in Education on the topic "Federal Aid to Parochial Schools," including some theological basis for separation of church and state. The next class was a seminar on Catholic and Protestant concepts of tradition. But instead of a seminar, the large room was jammed with students and faculty. I had been warned in advance by my letter of invitation: "The students and faculty are looking with a great deal of enthusiasm -- I believe that you will be the first faculty member of a non-Catholic seminary to speak here, so history -- and understanding -- is being made!"

During the question and answer period a student asked: "Were you born into the Methodist Church?" When I said, "Yes," he asked, "If you left the Methodist Church for another, what would it be?" I said, "The Quakers." Then he asked, "Why don't you leave?" My answer was, "There is still a lot I can learn from and contribute to the Methodist Church in terms of change."

After the class was over, the faculty went outside in the sunshine; some of them also went for a smoke. One professor took me aside and said, "Your answer to that question helped me. I have been considering leaving the Catholic Church." When I asked why, he said: "It's a terribly corrupt institution." We became good friends and the last letter I had from him in the early 1970s indicated that he was still in the Church.

That evening I met with the faculty and a small group of students in theology and philosophy to discuss pacifism. One professor just back from Rome said that pacifism was wrong. "If anyone tried to kill me or was involved in a killing, I feel I could, as a Christian, kill the offender." My response: "Then if you had been Stephen you would have killed the Apostle Paul." The faculty roared, but the professor kept raising questions. Not long afterward, he and some others on the faculty joined the Fellowship of Reconciliation. (Among the faculty were Fathers Earl Johnson, Ralph Sturm, Martin Pieke, and Rod Hindery.) When that faculty was disbanded by Bishop Charles Helmsing and forced to seek other positions, I helped two of them relocate.

On one other occasion several years later I was invited by the students of Conception for an evening lecture and discussion on pacifism.

In early 1965 I was invited to be the speaker at St. Benedict's Abbey in Atchison, Kansas, for their first experience in ecumenism. The *Kansas City Star* of February 16, 1965, said the Benedictine monks "were hosts to the Atchison Protestant Ministerial Alliance in an interesting display of ecumenism. In an unprecedented event, the Protestants were served dinner in the Abbey's refectory . . . More than 100 persons were at the meeting."

On a sabbatical trip to Europe in 1966 I visited a Dominican house or monastery in Holland to discuss the doctrine of the just war with some Dutch Catholic scholars. There I met Fr. Andre G. Dekker, a professor of philosophy. Upon the death of his father, he decided to come to the United States as a guest teacher or lecturer. I raised the question with the President and the faculty of St. Paul School of Theology where I was teaching, and shared his credentials with them. I was authorized to invite him to teach in the field of church history or historical theology. He had already come to America, had visited briefly with us in Kansas City, where he met the faculty, then went to Canada. I wrote him there in January 1969: "You have a position here beginning February 1 if you want it." He decided he wanted to stay in the field of philosophy and sought a post elsewhere.

Prior to the 1966 trip to Europe I attended the first large national demonstration in Washington against the Vietnam war. I was also invited to speak to a peace group at Catholic University, where for the first time I met Philip Berrigan. I believe this was before he had joined with his brother Dan (Berrigan) in the series of civilly disobedient demonstrations against war and conscription. He told me then that he had been reading *Current Issues,* an anti-war newsletter I wrote that went regularly to about a thousand people.

Subsequently I became acquainted with Dan Berrigan and many years later I invited Dan, Phil, and Sidney Lens to join in signing a letter to about fifty peace activists, including one Catholic bishop, to a Thanksgiving weekend conference in Washington in an effort to get all peace organizations engaged in a united campaign to ban nuclear weapons.

Kansas City is the home of the *National Catholic Reporter,* the liberal lay Roman Catholic weekly. When I went to Kansas City in 1960 I became acquainted with the editor, Robert G. Hoyt, and some others on the staff of what was then called *The Catholic Reporter.*

Upon occasion I wrote articles for the *NCR*. In 1968, Bishop Charles Helmsing of the Kansas City-St. Joseph Diocese, publicly condemned the *NCR*. It was a serious confrontation for the newspaper. I wrote a four-paragraph statement and sent it to leading Protestant clergy in Kansas City asking for their signatures. The statement expressed "our appreciation for and support of a free religious press just as we support and defend freedom of the secular press." The statement also said, "We have assumed that it was not an official organ of the Roman Catholic Church." In conclusion, the statement said, "*The National Catholic Reporter*, instead of undermining our respect for the Roman Catholic Church, has enhanced it by its devotion to freedom of expression, its irenic and objective handling of controversy and its creative reporting of the continuing renewal of the Church."

Fifty of Kansas City's leading clergy signed the statement, which I sent to Bishop Helmsing and to the editor, Bob Hoyt. Bob Hoyt asked me not to release the statement to the *Kansas City Star*. I complied, but sent a copy to the Catholic Press Association in New York, and received a copy of their statement which urged "the Bishops of the United States to join the Catholic Press Association in creating a competent forum for drawing up such guidelines for both bishop and journalist who are sincerely trying to carry out their respective responsibilities." The confrontation not only ended but both Bob Hoyt and Bishop Helmsing wrote me expressing appreciation for our statement.

Shortly after the ending of the Second Vatican Council, I participated in Kansas City in a regularly scheduled ecumenical dialogue of five Protestants, five Jews, and five Roman Catholics. One of the five Catholics was a priest named William Baum, subsequently a Cardinal in Rome in charge of the Educational Secretariat. I suggested that we deal with controversial issues, beginning with separation of church and state. Baum took the lead in saying that he was sure his Catholic colleagues would agree with the position I took. Throughout our discussion we could find virtually no disagreement.

Bill Baum and I became good friends. I invited him to speak at our School of Theology, and we got together on other occasions. But after he became a bishop, he ignored my letter of congratulation and other letters and took an institutional position on aid to church schools quite different from what he said he believed in our group. When I went to Argentina in 1969 to teach as a visiting professor in a Buenos Aires Faculty of Theology, Bob Hoyt gave me press credentials and asked me to write some stories for the *National Catholic Reporter.* Again in 1977, when I went to Africa on sabbatical leave, I carried press credentials from Arthur Jones, the new editor. Twelve of my stories written in various parts of Africa, including Ethiopia, Kenya, Zambia, Rhodesia and South Africa, were published in *NCR.*

On a number of occasions I lectured at Incarnate Word College in San Antonio, Texas, where one of my books, *Liberation Ethics,* had been used as a textbook. And in 1976 I was invited to give the summer commencement address on the topic, "Education and Liberation."

In 1979 I was scheduled to be a speaker at the national Pax Christi conference. My topic was to be nuclear power and war. Pax Christi is an international Catholic peace organization. Although I had been asked months in advance of the October conference, I did not learn until September that Father Gerald Senecal, the President of Benedictine College in Atchison, Kansas, where the conference was to be held, had told Pax Christi authorities that I would not be permitted on the campus.

Angie O'Gorman, a friend of mine who was the local Pax Christi coordinator, said, according to the September 14 *National Catholic Reporter,* that Senecal told her that "Swomley was 'anti-church' and a 'bigot.' O'Gorman said Senecal told her Swomley could not appear on campus because of Swomley's views on separation of church and state and abortion. O'Gorman asked for specific examples of writings or speeches by Swomley proving the allegations of bigotry, but none was provided."

Gordon Zahn, a friend of many years and a prominent Catholic sociologist, who was also scheduled to lead a workshop, told *NCR,* "If they are characterizing him as a bigot they are mistaken. I do not consider him anti-Catholic, though we differ on certain topics."

The first intimation that I had been banned came not from any Pax Christi leader but from a staff member of the *National Catholic Reporter,* who asked me for a statement for their next issue. I decided not to make an "off the cuff" statement, but to give the *NCR* a written one. I said, in part:

> The withdrawal of the invitation comes as a surprise but not as an affront. My surprise is because I had assumed the term "Catholic" describes an inclusiveness that tolerates difference. I have the greatest respect for Pax Christi and its leadership, so I don't want to do or say anything to harm it. The world needs all the peace activity it can muster. Pax Christi is making a very significant contribution and will do so whether I attend the conference in Atchison or not.
>
> There are, without doubt, people in Pax Christi who are concerned about free speech and the desirability of dialogue with those from other traditions who hold differing points of view on some questions. If they have been unable to persuade the college president, Father Senecal, that Pax Christi should be able to determine whom they will invite to speak, nothing that I say will be persuasive.

I went on to indicate my belief that "conscience as well as medical judgment should determine whether abortion is to be chosen, just as I believe conscience should determine whether anyone prepares for or participates in nuclear or other war." I also indicated that I would not have raised either the abortion or separation of church and state issues at the conference "if only because I respect religious convictions that differ from mine." There were other items in my statement, but the *National Catholic Reporter* unfortunately printed only my first two sentences. I did, however, furnish a copy of the statement to Pax Christi leaders. As a result I received a letter of regret from Bishop Thomas Gumbleton of Detroit.

Pax Christi leaders acquiesced in Father Senecal's ultimatum. Sister Mary Evelyn Jegen, the national coordinator for Pax Christi and subsequently national chairperson for the Fellowship of Reconciliation, sought to sooth any ruffled feelings by telling me she would invite me to speak at the following year's conference, though in fact she did not. I was also asked to come to Atchison to meet a workshop in a motel off campus. I declined, stating that this was the way Christians used to treat black speakers in the 1930s who were not welcome on the campus or in the church.

The November 2 *National Catholic Reporter* in a report from the conference said: "The Benedictine College ban of the respected nuclear disarmament expert was an issue that popped up constantly at the Pax Christi U.S.A. national assembly here last month. It was the item of discussion both for participants and organizers whose meetings were almost entirely tied up with how to deal with it. Even students protested the ban."

Pax Christi's executive council with two dissenting votes, one of them Bishop Gumbleton, according to a report to me from a member of the Council, issued a statement censuring Father Senecal in which they said the Council "profoundly regrets the decision taken by the president of the host college." The statement also said the problem showed "a failure in the Council to handle the situation in a concerted fashion."

According to the *NCR,* Joseph Fahey, the new Pax Christi executive council chairman, said he was going to drop out of the conference altogether in protest, but decided to attend "to keep negotiations with Senecal going and to keep Pax Christi together." The *NCR* also said, "Swomley, a Methodist who is called by Fahey 'more Catholic than many of us,' said, 'Unless there was a recognition of differences in faith, there is no real ecumenism possible.'"

A Protestant periodical, *The Christian Century,* reported briefly the ban on my speaking but did report Father Senecal's charges. As a result there were a number of letters from Roman Catholic nuns in the November 7, 1979, *Century.* Four Kansas City nuns, Sisters Marie Frances Kenoyer, Mary McNellis, Barbara Doak, and Shirley Koritnik, objected to the characterization of me as a "bigot." Sister Margaret Ellen Traxler of Chicago wrote, "I am indignant over his rejection by the President of Benedictine College. . . . The very stones of Benedictine College must cry out protesting the slander against John Swomley."

Unfortunately this Pax Christi affair was not an isolated incident. As chair of the lecture committee at Saint Paul School of Theology I had invited Bishop Leroy T. Matthiesen of Amarillo, Texas, to deliver a series of lectures at our school. He had opposed the manufacture of parts for nuclear weapons in a factory in his diocese. He was delighted to come, said his calendar was clear, and asked me to clear it with Bishop Joseph Sullivan of Kansas City. When Bishop Sullivan could not speak to me, I left a message with his receptionist. Soon thereafter I received a letter from Bishop Matthiesen canceling the engagement and also stating that there would be no point in trying to reschedule the lectures. Bishop Sullivan may have believed he was inflicting some retribution for my position on church and state. However, some two hundred theological students and faculty were deprived of hearing a creative Catholic peace personality and the Bishop was deprived of a very substantial honorarium.

The previous Kansas City bishop, Charles Helmsing, had a rule regarding me. He told leaders of Catholic organizations that they could invite me to speak on war and other social issues, but not on separation of church and state. I had no rule with respect to Bishop Helmsing, whom I liked and respected. At my invitation he spoke to a Saint Paul Assembly March 25, 1965.

In January 1985 I was to brief a Witness for Peace group going on their first visit to Nicaragua during the war there. Sister Kathleen Kenny, who had invited me, told me she had to cancel the invitation at the request of the pastor of St. Charles Roman Catholic Church in Kansas City, presumably because of my stand on reproductive freedom for women.

My conclusion from long experience is that many priests, sisters, and laity welcome non-Catholic speakers and friendships with Protestants, Jews and non-church people in spite of these persons' rejection of some or all Roman Catholic teaching. But some others are more concerned with ideology than with persons or with friendly relations, and test everyone's acceptability by their views on abortion or aid to parochial schools or some other Vatican position.

My positive relationship with Roman Catholic leaders continues to this day. In the early 1980s, after a pioneer visit to Nicaragua and other Central American countries where the C.I.A. and other U.S. forces were active, I joined with Tom Fox, the present editor of the *National Catholic Reporter,* in forming a Kansas City regional Committee on Central America. And in 1993 when the U.S. was threatening a strike and nuclear war against North Korea, I formed the American Committee on Korea which includes six well-known Roman Catholics among its thirty-seven members. On my first trip to North Korea in 1994, well before the United States and North

Korea had begun to resolve their conflict, I visited the small Catholic and the larger Presbyterian churches in Pyongyang with government officials to emphasize the concern and appreciation of our Committee for acceptance by the North Korean government of religious participation in the life of the country.

Despite cancellation of speaking engagements and rejection of manuscripts by Catholic periodicals that formerly published my work, I remain convinced that it is important to work together with progressive Catholics on mutual goals, while opposing the political agenda of right-wing Catholic organizations, including those measures promoted at the highest level in the Vatican.

Chapter 2
Life in the Methodist Church

Although my experiences as a Methodist have been rewarding on the whole, life in the Methodist Church has not always been easy. After I graduated from the Boston University School of Theology, I was told I would be denied admission to the Central Pennsylvania Annual Conference. The Annual Conference is somewhat like a labor union. Prospective ministers are on trial for a period of two years as apprentices, but once admitted to membership in the Conference, are guaranteed a job in some church or church agency. Theoretically, the bishops have no power to determine membership, but some exercise more power than the rules of the church permit. Bishop Adna Leonard of Pittsburgh was such a "dictator."

Bishop Leonard, while President of the Methodist Board of Education, had decided to dismiss two Methodist ministers, Blaine Kirkpatrick and Owen Geer, who headed youth work in the Church in the U.S. He felt they were too "radical." They had been helpful in forming the semi-autonomous National Council of Methodist Youth, to which I have already referred. Their dismissal was accepted by the Board and they took other posts in the Methodist Church. When Bishop Leonard appeared at a large National Conference of Methodist Youth in 1938, I cross-examined him after his speech before more than a thousand young people. I questioned his exercise of power in dismissing these two men. He never forgave me. Although he was not the bishop in Central Pennsylvania, he exercised enough influence there that I was warned by a district superintendent, Lester Welliver, not even to seek membership.

My second rebuff was at the hands of Bishop G. Bromley Oxnam. There was a rule in the Methodist Discipline that one must serve two years in a church under the supervision of a District Superintendent. Bishop Oxnam, who was opposed to pacifism, wanted me to leave the staff of the pacifist Fellowship of Reconciliation during World War II and serve a church. His son, who had entered the military chaplaincy, was given an exception to this rule. Bishop Oxnam, however, did not believe a ministry to conscientious objectors, interned Japanese Americans, etc. was on a par with the chaplaincy if one worked for the Fellowship of Reconciliation.

My friend Lester Auman, a district superintendent in the New York East Conference, asked me in 1955 why I had not joined the Conference. When I explained, he said: "In our Conference we don't permit bishops to have anything to do with conference membership." So after the necessary interviews, exams and a two-thirds vote required by my age, I was admitted and ordained.

My third turn-down came after I was teaching at Saint Paul School of Theology in Kansas City. After teaching there for several years I asked Bishop Eugene Frank to transfer me into the Missouri West Conference. Although he was personally friendly to me, he was very wary because of radical positions and actions I had taken, many of which were reported in the Kansas City papers. He took no action on my request for transfer. A year later I renewed my request, with the same result. Somewhat later I asked a third time. He said, "I will consult the Cabinet." I knew that the bishop did not need to consult anyone and had the power to transfer. This time I did not wait but asked the bishop of Kansas, W. Macferrin Stowe, for a transfer into the Kansas East Conference. By return mail I received an enthusiastic letter welcoming me into the Conference.

There were similar experiences in local churches in Greater Kansas City where our family attended. At St. John's United Methodist the pastor, John Guice, invited me to preach a sermon during his absence. In the sermon was an illustration about racial discrimination against a black family. The chairman of the Board made it quite clear that any discussion of changing race relations was unwelcome in that church. On a subsequent Sunday a member of the church, in a loud voice after the benediction, as people were beginning to leave, asked the pastor why he permitted a "Communist" to attend that church. After other unpleasant episodes, and the fact that St. John's refused to join most other Methodist churches in calling for a City Ordinance against discrimination, we left that church and my wife joined Old Mission United Methodist Church, which was nearer to where we lived.

Some months later in 1966 the lay leader of that church, a lawyer named Sherman L. Gibson, and the pastor, Fred Ackman, asked if I would have lunch with them. In the course of the lunch, Gibson asked me to "keep a respectful silence" in Old Mission and to be "more judicious" in my public speaking and action elsewhere. The pastor did not share Gibson's views. Gibson was particularly upset at my views on foreign policy and said that ministers should leave discussion on foreign policy to laymen such as himself. I asked him if he had ever had a course on foreign policy in law school; I knew the answer in advance as law schools do not offer such courses. Then I told him that with a degree in political science and a theological degree including social ethics, I taught such courses in our School of Theology. Gibson nevertheless persisted in telling me that if I were vocal in the church, twenty percent of the congregation would quietly disappear.

My experience at Saint Paul School of Theology was quite different. The President, Don W. Holter, was not only a real believer in academic freedom, but also welcomed my strong role in social action. I feel fortunate in having had a long relationship with him as President and as a friend. He later became Bishop Holter. The faculty without exception were also very supportive, even though many disagreed with some of the positions I took. The students, many of whom came form conservative "Bible Belt" backgrounds, with a few exceptions were challenged by a wholly different approach to religion. Perhaps as many as one-third began to look at war, foreign policy, economics and other problems in our society from a more progressive or radical perspective.

One of my early experiences with the faculty and students was at a debate with the Johnson County, Kansas, Civil Defense administrator, Leighton Spadone. Spadone decided to erect a loud Civil Defense siren on the property of the Cherokee Christian Church, to go off whenever Spadone wanted. The pastor, Rev. Tom Underwood, who opposed this, arranged a public debate between Mr. Spadone and me in the church on March 10, 1961. Most of the faculty and a number of students at the school as well as church members and prominent leaders in the county attended. One prominent businessman phoned Dr. Holter before the debate to ask if he was sure I was not a Communist.

Mr. Spadone was neither a master of the subject of nuclear weapons nor of civil defense, nor able to deal with my arguments. While I was speaking he became angry, ran to the back of the room, shouting epithets at me. Then as I continued speaking, he started back up the aisle after me. Sitting on the front row on a corner seat was a huge six-foot ex-Army sergeant, John Krivo, one of my students who did not share my anti-war convictions. John blocked the aisle with his body, and said to Spadone, "You aren't going anywhere. You're not going to lay a hand on him."

The room eventually quieted down and the debate resumed. After the debate and the subsequent discussion it aroused, the plan to erect a siren on church property was never consummated.

It was not long after I was teaching in Kansas City that I discovered how influential a theology professor might be, even while holding radical political views. National church boards and bishops valued expertise and I was one of only a handful of theology professors with a degree in political science as well as in theology. There were even fewer with experience in the peace and other social action movements. I was elected to the General Board of Christian Social Concerns and called upon frequently to testify before Congressional committees on issues related to peace, conscription, and church-state relations. One of the tasks given to me was to defend a statement by the 1968 General Conference affirming "the right of non-violent civil disobedience in extreme cases as a viable option in a democracy and as a sometime requirement of Christians. . . . "

That statement on civil disobedience had been recommended by the Board of Social Concerns and after its adoption was challenged by the conservative Southeastern Jurisdictional Conference as being in conflict with one of the articles of the Church's Constitution. Briefs for and against the statement were submitted to the Judicial Council of the United Methodist Church for a decision. That Council upheld the constitutionality of the General Conference statement. One of the members of the Council was Leon Hickman, general counsel of the Aluminum Corporation of America (Alcoa) and chairman of the Council's finance committee, who did not share many of my views.

I was delighted, therefore, to get his letter of November 15, 1968 which included the following paragraph:

I want to extend a word of congratulation on the brief that you filed with the Judicial Council on the constitutionality of the statement on nonviolent civil disobedience endorsed by the General Conference. Your statement supported the General Conference resolution with a biblical, ethical, and legal foundation that we got from no other supporting statement. You were quite convincing and we were greatly helped.

One of the few humorous episodes involving a Methodist bishop occurred in 1961-1962 as a result of a Kansas Council of Churches Committee Report on Civil Defense. I was a member of the Committee, which made the report after months of study. The report was largely drafted by Gilbert Murphy, a Presbyterian minister in Gardner, Kansas, and myself. Robert Meneilly and other prominent clergy were on the Committee. The seven-page report dealt with scientific, psychological and financial aspects of civil defense, quoting responsible national authorities. The report at one point said: "Perhaps the most devastating psychological effect of the Civil Defense program has been the name-calling campaign which is resulting from the program. Some of our most respected citizens are receiving" a pro-Communist label by those enthusiastic about C.D. Any person objecting to the C.D. program is apt to be called "'pink' or a 'red' and in one case it is reliably reported that the F.B.I. has been called in to investigate an objector."

When the report was presented to the Kansas Council of Churches Assembly by Gilbert Murphy I was seated beside the Methodist Bishop of Kansas, O. Eugene Slater, a gentle pastoral person who I believe was at one time a member of the Fellowship of Reconciliation. When the vote to approve the report was taken, there were only two people who stood in the affirmative, Gilbert Murphy and myself. I turned and looked directly down at Bishop Slater, who after a moment's hesitation stood up. Then every Methodist in the room got to his feet, and before long those from other denominations rose, until it appeared to be a unanimous vote, or nearly so. I never asked the bishop, whom all of us admired and respected, whether he had been uncertain, or had not wanted originally to influence the vote!

In 1967 at a meeting of a committee of the Division of Peace and World Order of the Board of Christian Social Concerns and a committee from the Women's Division and the Division of World

Mission, a decision was made to "set up a working party or task force to prepare" a "document suitable for wide use in the church which would analyze the problem of revolution and counter-revolution in our contemporary world" and also deal with the Church and War. According to the Minutes, "John Swomley was asked to prepare a prospectus by December 31, 1967, on the basis of which a select interdisciplinary group would work to develop a summary statement" for General Conference "and a longer study and strategy document for wider study in the Church." I prepared the prospectus as requested, and was invited to serve on the interdisciplinary task force. The finished document, "The Christian Faith and War in the Nuclear Age," was the result of papers prepared by the twelve members of the General Conference Commission and four extensive meetings. The final draft, for which I was largely responsible, was issued as a study document for the whole church, and preceded by more than a decade the Roman Catholic Bishops Pastoral Letter, and the subsequent statement by the United Methodist Bishops.

During the quadrennial period 1964 to 1968 I was a member of the General Conference Commission to study Church-State Relations. The Commission believed in separation of church and state, but the staff member, W. Astor Kirk, a black political scientist, seemed to believe in government aid to religious institutions. As a result, when he prepared the draft report it indicated that church-related social welfare agencies "should have the same privileges of access to government resources as all other private non-profit social welfare agencies." It also asked "Cooperation between agencies of government and non-public educational institutions, including those that have formal relations with religious bodies." The report also included a statement that "the cooperation referred to may take the form of governmental support of special purpose educational programs that bear a clear relation to a legitimate objective of public policy."

Since education in general is a "legitimate objective of public policy," it became obvious that all programs of education, short of instruction in catechism, might qualify for governmental support. When I told Kirk this was not what the Commission had decided and charged him with altering our decision, he said he had lost the draft we made and written what he thought was our position. I objected to Bishop Raymond Grant, who served on the Study Commission.

There was no one on the Commission other than myself who was prepared for a hostile encounter with a determined black staff member over the Report to General Conference. Therefore I chose a different procedure. I joined with Dean M. Kelley, Director for Civil and Religious Liberty of the National Council of Churches, and Philip Wogaman, professor of social ethics at Wesley Theological Seminary in Washington, D.C., in preparing "a systematic exposition of an alternative view."

Our alternative view affirmed religious liberty, including rights of conscience for those who could not participate in any war and those who could not participate in a particular war. We also objected to "placing 'religious' conscience in a preferential position over 'non-religious' conscience." We proposed strict guidelines for health and welfare agencies founded by churches without regard to religious proselytizing, and opposed public aid to church-related schools and colleges, as well as public prayer and devotional services in the public schools.

I accepted the responsibility for mimeographing and mailing our 18-page statement to every one of the hundreds of delegates to General Conference in advance of that meeting, and for raising the money for the purpose. Although our alternative view was not adopted as such, the United Methodist Church has from that day to this generally accepted our objectives. As recently as 1987 I was consulted on the proposed document on Religious Liberty adopted by the General Conference in 1988.

Five years after the 1968 General Conference adopted the statement, "We do not support the expansion or the strengthening of private schools with public funds," I was asked to appear before the House Ways and Means Committee on March 23, 1973, to represent the United Methodist position by opposing tuition tax credits for religious schools.

On another occasion in 1971, I represented the position of the United Methodist General Conference before the Senate Armed Services Committee in opposition to the continuation of the draft and for a voluntary armed force. Also in 1971 when the Council of Bishops was "seeking to develop a 'peace emphasis' for the United Methodist Church in 1972, I was asked to read the preliminary position paper and react to it. A letter from Bishop James Armstrong June 2, 1971, said, "I have received many responses to the 'preliminary position paper.' None has approached yours in terms of incisive and legitimate direction. . . . Surely much of your material will be incorporated in the document before it comes to the General Conference."

In the early 1960s I served as a consultant to the Division of World Missions of the Board of Missions dealing with various issues such as revolutionary movements, Communism, and problems to be discussed in a convocation on social concerns to be held in November, 1963, in Europe with representatives from various countries. My ideas of course were not always accepted. I proposed without success that the Division of World Missions bring key Latin American youth and young adults to the U.S. for intensive education related to problems of Communism, guerrilla and other revolutionary movements and the whole process of liberation which some years later became a major issue in Latin America. I was also unsuccessful in persuading the Board leadership to adopt a program of missions to social movements in addition to missions to geographic areas. These movements included Communist, African and South American liberation groups, environmental, labor, and other groups.

Also, at the suggestion of the General Board of Christian Social Concerns, I participated in a project that contributed to the legalization of abortion. In 1971 the publication "Abortion: A Human Choice" carried my research on abortion and civil liberty. This was before the *Roe v. Wade* decision of the Supreme Court.

In Kansas City I was also active on issues of concern to the Church. During the Presidential campaign of Lyndon Johnson and Barry Goldwater in 1964, Republican headquarters in Kansas City was distributing the right-wing book, *None Dare Call It Treason*, by John Stormer, which attacked various groups, including the churches. I prepared a brief statement for circulation to Methodist ministers in Greater Kansas City for their signatures. In it was this paragraph:

Many of us have criticized the churches in Germany for remaining silent when the Nazis began to undermine democratic institutions in Germany and to attack an important religious group for alleged Communism and internationalism. We cannot stand idly by while our own church and the National Council of Churches are similarly and falsely attacked by irresponsible but organized extremist voices.

That statement was signed by seventy-four Methodist ministers. After several attempts to persuade leaders at Republican headquarters to withdraw the book, I invited these ministers, the faculty of our School of Theology and theological students, to join me in picketing the Republican Party headquarters. On October 22, more than eighty Methodist ministers and theological students moved in an elliptical circle with signs of protest, while a Methodist district superintendent, Kenneth Johnson, and I were inside the headquarters asking them to stop distributing the book. They refused.

The following day the ministers' protest dominated the front page of the *Kansas City Times* and was carried on all television stations. Republican leaders counterattacked and accused the ministers of a purely political act. On Sunday, October 25, the *Kansas City Star* carried a vigorous statement of support written by the Missouri Methodist Bishop, Eugene Frank, and another statement signed by forty-seven leading non-Methodist clergy, including Episcopal Bishop Edward R. Welles and Walter N. Johnson, a bishop of the Reorganized Church of Latter Day Saints. For five days running the incident was given extensive publicity in the press. William F. Case, dean of the School of Theology, said the Methodist Church got more publicity than from a month of revival meetings!

There were many attacks on the ministers. Some members left churches of pastors who participated. Three prominent Republicans who served on the executive committee of the Board of Trustees of the Saint Paul School of Theology demanded my resignation from the faculty, and persisted in this every year thereafter at all meetings of the Board and its executive committee. I am glad to say that their efforts were resisted by Dr. Don Holter, on the grounds of academic freedom, and not seconded by other members of the Board.

There were many positive reactions. Rabbi Morris Margolies of the largest Jewish Congregation, a Conservative one, phoned me to ask, "Are you hurting?" He said, "If you are, these are not just idle words of consolation. If you have suffered financially as a seminary, I want to help get financial support." I thanked him and told him I thought we could weather the storm. We became close friends thereafter, and he appeared at my retirement celebration in 1985 to make a public statement on behalf of the Jewish community.

Another source of support at that time came from Charles Blackmar, President of the Jackson County Republican Club, and much later a member of the Supreme Court of Missouri. He wrote the Republican National Committee and received a letter indicating that they had no policy endorsing or promoting *None Dare Call It Treason*.

In spite of the various sources of support, I became a controversial figure in Kansas City Methodism and almost never was invited to speak in Methodist churches thereafter. Even Kenneth Johnson, whose church our family attended for a number of years, never invited me to speak even to a Sunday School class.

One other source of controversy in Kansas City is worth noting. There was a Methodist Inner City Parish serving both poor blacks and whites. After a succession of white pastors, the Rev. Philip Lawson became the Director of the Parish. During his tenure there were charges that he permitted the Black Panthers to store weapons in a parish building and that he supported the Panthers in other ways. I had known the Lawson family for years and knew it as committed to non-violence. However, some of Phil Lawson's closest white friends, including a theological school colleague of mine, who were not pacifists, condoned violence.

Hubert Johnson, chief of racial intelligence in the Kansas City region for the F.B.I., phoned to ask me about Phil Lawson. I assured him that Phil was neither a Communist nor an advocate of violence. Johnson had phoned at the time Lawson was to appear before the House Unamerican Activities Committee. I told him that I knew the Lawson family in Ohio and that they were pacifists. I believe he accepted my judgment.

In 1970 during the Vietnam war, while he was on a two-week visit to Vietnam, including a trip to Hanoi in North Vietnam, Lawson issued a statement directed to black American troops: "To My Black Brothers in the U.S. Forces in Vietnam" in which he said, about the Vietnamese people:

Brothers, surely you can see that these people are our brothers and sisters. . . . Black brothers, do not rape the country for the benefit of business and military interests!

Withdraw! You can refuse to rape; by refusing to rape you can maintain your humanity. Black brothers, do not kill women and children. You can shoot over their heads.

There were additional strong words which were reported in Kansas City. These words obviously disturbed some Methodists in Kansas City. Yet presumably all Christians accept the fact that all people, including Vietnamese, are their brothers and sisters, and that non-combatants should not be killed.

There were demands for the removal of Lawson from his position as Director of the Inner City Parish. In the meantime the Board of Directors of the Inner City Parish met on October 13, defended the right of any individual to speak his conscience, and affirmed the continuance of Lawson as Director. Bishop Frank called for a special session of the Missouri West Conference on the recommendation of his cabinet of district superintendents, who also urged that Lawson be limited to serving just one of the churches in the Inner City Parish. The Conference Board of Ordained Ministry met on October 27 and recommended that Lawson voluntarily "locate," which meant continuing as a minister without serving a church.

At one point a West Coast black bishop, Charles Golden, whom I knew well, phoned me about the situation. Golden and I had attended a Chicago conference on Black Power and had a genuine mutual respect. He indicated that the Lawson matter would be discussed at the next meeting of the Council of Bishops in Portland, Oregon, and asked for an objective summary of the problem. I remember that our conversation lasted an hour and a half. I did not know what happened at the Portland meeting, but noted that Bishop Frank's stance thereafter was a moderating one.

My next involvement came in March, 1970, when seminary president Don Holter called me in to his office to indicate that the Bishop of Kansas, W. McFerrin Stowe, and Missouri bishop Eugene Frank wanted to issue a public statement putting an end to the controversy, which had also led to public hearings on the Kansas City Panthers before the House Committee on Internal Security in Washington in early March. Holter told me the bishops wanted me to prepare a broad policy statement that would be acceptable to both black and white Christians that would repudiate violence but would respect all parties to the controversy and they wanted it available promptly.

I wrote a 13-paragraph statement which the bishops issued to the press. It was carried in full on the front page and page two of the *Kansas City Star* March 15, 1970, and did effectively end the controversy. The statement said:

> White Christians should ask forgiveness for the centuries of violence inflicted on our black brothers . . . We repudiate both violence and the threats of violence because these are not the way to increase respect for human life. Specifically we reject as incompatible with the Gospel, the philosophy, statements and actions of the Black Panthers which advocate or encourage the use of violence, the stockpiling of weapons and intimidation of other citizens, whether black or white.
>
> We do so not because the Panthers are black or seek drastic changes in the American scene, but for the same reasons we cannot accept the philosophy, statements, and actions of the Minutemen, the Ku Klux Klan, or other white groups that seek by violence to form society after their own image.

On the other hand the statement justified "Black Power" as intended "to achieve full participation in our political, social, religious and economic life." It dissociated black power from violence and noted that violence "generally stimulates such hatred and antagonism as to thwart the kind of mutual respect that is essential to equal participation in our common life."

My participation in the formation of policy in the Kansas East Conference and even upon occasion in Missouri was frequently effective, in the writing of letters or statements for various bishops, sometimes speaking on policy matters on the floor of Annual Conference. But in general the ordinary parish minister in Missouri and Kansas was hesitant to invite me to speak to his local congregation.

Fortunately I was invited more often to speak in other churches-- Lutheran, Presbyterian, Unitarian-Universalist, United Church of Christ, Disciples of Christ, and occasionally Roman Catholic.

On two occasions I was asked to serve as interim minister. I served for about six months in a Maysville, Missouri, church and for twenty-two months in the 800-member Salem United Church of Christ in Higginsville, Missouri. In fact, I am still listed as a recognized supply pastor in those two denominations.

Outside of Missouri and Kansas, of course, I was frequently invited to speak in Methodist churches and districts and Conference events.

Chapter 3
More Church-State Battles

The conflict over Roman Catholic efforts to get tax support for parochial schools and other church institutions was rooted in two facts. The first was a *de facto* Protestant establishment for many years, evident in such activities as Protestant prayers or religious observances in many public schools. Legally this came to an end with the Supreme Court decisions in 1962 and 1963 which banned both school-sponsored Bible reading and vocal prayer in the public schools. Most public schools in the Midwest and West did not have such devotional services before that decision, but others, in the East and the South, did.[1] However, some schools continue to violate the Supreme Court decisions even into the 1990s. Obviously Roman Catholic leaders did not want their school children subjected to Protestant influence in public schools. This created much of the drive for parochial schools in the late half of the nineteenth and earlier half of the twentieth centuries.

The second fact was a Catholic Church political position first set forth by Pope Leo XIII (1878-1903): "The State must not only 'have care for religion,' but recognize the true religion professed by the Catholic Church. It is a thoroughly logical position. If the State is under moral compulsion to profess and promote religion, it is obviously obliged to profess and promote only the religion that is true; for no individual, no group of individuals, no society, no State is justified in supporting error or in according to error the same recognition as to truth."[2] This obviously created Protestant and Jewish opposition to Catholic efforts to force non-Catholics to pay taxes for Catholic institutions.

---

[1] John M. Swomley, "Myths About Voluntary School Prayer," *Washburn University Law Journal*, Vol. 35, Spring 1996.

[2] John A. Ryan and Francis J. Boland, *Catholic Principles of Politics* (New York: Macmillan, 1960), pp. 313, 314.

The Second Vatican Council (1962-1963) included among its Decrees a "Declaration on Religious Liberty," widely hailed at the time by many Protestant leaders. However, it affirms "traditional Catholic doctrine on the moral duty of men and societies toward the true religion and toward the one Church of Christ" which "subsists in the Catholic and Apostolic Church. . . . " Other groups may receive "special civil recognition." It perpetuates the claim that religious liberty for the Roman Catholic Church is grounded in divine law and the special status given to her as the one true church, whereas for non-Catholics the basis for liberty is limited to belief in human dignity or "civil right." Nowhere in the document does it speak of religious liberty within the church.

The Jesuit weekly *America* said, in its October 2, 1965, editorial, "It is perhaps necessary to remind Americans that the Council is not about to enact the First Amendment of the United States Constitution as a Catholic Doctrine."

The Vatican Council further restricted religious liberty by its "Declaration on Christian Education," which "reminds Catholic parents of the duty of entrusting their children to Catholic schools." It also demanded "that public subsidies are paid out in such a way that parents are truly free to choose" a Catholic school. It further says that the Roman Catholic "family, which has the primary duty of imparting education, needs the help of the whole community," which it defines as a civic duty "to give them aid and moreover, as the common good demands, to build schools and institutions." In other words, it wants Catholics to send their children to parochial schools, Protestants, Jews, Muslims and non-believers to pay taxes to support those parents who send their children to Catholic or other sectarian day church schools under the deceptive guise of "benefits to children."

The impact of these two declarations is to leave to all the bishops in each country the decision whether to demand government support of their church schools, and to what extent they will support religious liberty for others as a "civil right." In the United States the bishops as a group subsequently filed an *amicus* brief to the U.S. Supreme Court through the U.S. Catholic Conference in the 1983 *Mueller v. Allen* case putting them squarely on record as opposing the American concept of separation of church and state on matters having to do with aid for Roman Catholic institutions.

Mueller v. Allen was a case involving claims by parochial school parents for income tax deductions for tuition, textbooks and transportation for children attending elementary and secondary schools. Although the statute was cleverly drawn to permit parents of public school children also to claim such deductions, public school parents do not pay for tuition, textbooks and transportation costs except in a rare circumstance such as attendance by a student in another district. Nevertheless, the Supreme Court validated these parochial school expense deductions. The U.S. Catholic Conference *amicus* brief went before the judges on this case to attack the entire principle of separation of church and state.

This is not an indication that Roman Catholics in general oppose separation of church and state. In fact, there is every indication that they do not follow the bishops' leadership in seeking to re-interpret or destroy the "establishment clause" of the First Amendment, which stipulates that "Congress shall make no law respecting an establishment of religion, or prohibiting the free exercise thereof." The Supreme Court has rightly interpreted that to mean that that government may not sponsor or finance any religion in particular or religion in general and may not prefer one or some religions over others or over non-religion.

However, the tremendous publicity given to Vatican II reforms at other points, plus the fact that few Protestant or Jewish clergy ever read the texts of Vatican II's Declarations, led to a considerable romanticism. Many thought the Catholic Church would no longer press for taxpayer money for their church institutions. They were mistaken.

After the end of Vatican II there was a big push nationwide for aid to parochial schools. I became involved in the conflict over aid to such schools in 1963 when Don W. Holter, the President of Saint Paul School of Theology where I taught, asked me to represent him and the school before Missouri legislative committees in opposing legislation for free bus transportation to parochial schools. Dr. Holter had been a missionary in the Philippines and seen and experienced the impact of a Catholic culture on schools, hospitals and non-Catholics in general.

Support for the bill for bus transportation came from Citizens for Educational Freedom (C.E.F.), a national lay group organized in St. Louis, to secure aid for parochial schools through vouchers to parents. Bus transportation was the beginning effort of what is called the "child benefit" theory that proponents believed eventually would lead to total aid to church schools.

In brief I told the legislative committees that transportation is aid to the school rather than the child. Originally schools were established on a community basis and hence within walking distance. "Bus transportation," I said, "made it possible for fewer school buildings to serve wider geographical areas, and therefore aids the school system. It was not a safety measure or public obligation, because it transports only for distances over a mile or mile and a half, and does not pick up students within walking distance, even if they have to pass hazardous intersections."

As an alternative I proposed larger income tax deductions for those contributing to religious educational and charitable institutions, or free public bus transportation for *all* children of school age to be used anywhere or every day. The Roads and Highways Committee rejected the bus transportation proposal and it was not reported out.

However, it came up again and again, and before the elections of November 1966, Catholic organizations openly engaged in efforts to influence the election of local and state officials. Candidates for the state legislature were judged by their position for or against aid to parochial schools; sample ballots were sent to Catholic adults; and even judges who did not agree with the C.E.F. position had a "No" recommendation where the ballot asked if they were to be retained in office. Catholics were also asked to oppose a tax increase for public schools because it might encourage students to transfer from private to public schools.

Although the Knights of Columbus, Catholic superintendents of schools and Catholic P.T.A.s took the above position, the *Catholic Reporter,* which was noted for its independent stand, endorsed the public school levy and deplored the circulation of lists for or against candidates.

Protestant groups reacted, and although the public school tax levy lost, too few parochial school candidates were elected to change the legislature's majority against it.

Then, in rapid succession, Catholic legislators in Missouri introduced bills to provide free textbooks for parochial schools; tuition reimbursement payments for parents with children in parochial schools; the provision of auxiliary services such as testing, teacher-counseling, remedial reading, speech correction, "and such other services as may be determined by the legislature." One bill was directed at "all free public libraries" to "provide textbooks for each student in any school in the state."

Some of these bills were identical in wording with those in other states, suggesting a central strategy for eroding separation of church and state.

I not only appeared before legislative committees in Missouri but prepared fact sheets for other opponents to use. In the meantime Hugh Wamble, an excellent church-state scholar, came to Kansas City to teach at Midwest Baptist Theological Seminary, making it possible for me to give attention to other states. In 1968 I went to Michigan to assist "Citizens to Advance Public Education" (CAPE) in their struggle against the drive by Christian Reformed and Roman Catholic schools to divert public school funds to their own budgets.

At a conference to launch CAPE's campaign in February 1968 I said, "If sectarian religious education serves a public function, then church schools that operate on Saturdays, Sundays and in the summer are equally entitled to receive state tuition grants for their pupils. But under our system of government, religious education is not a public function. The test of whether a subject in a parochial school is secular is the teacher. Will parochial schools abandon the practice of hiring teachers of their own faith for all of their so-called secular subjects? Will they hire humanists, atheists, Jews, Protestants, without any examination of their religious beliefs? Or is public money to be used in a school where there is a religious test for teaching?"

I asked, "If a bill is introduced in the legislature with a serious chance of passage, it should be amended so that any school eligible for state funds via tuition grants must be open to the general public without racial or religious discrimination. And no member of the teaching staff should be chosen or employed on the basis of race, religion or national origin."

During a number of visits to Michigan I debated Christian Reformed educators as well as Catholic priests. Probably the most significant debate was February 13, 1964, in the Fountain Street Church in Grand Rapids, with Father Virgil Blum, S.J., assistant professor of political science at Marquette University, and the chief spokesman for Citizens for Educational Freedom. The church was filled with over a thousand people.

In the course of the debate I asked if "legislators would be acting responsibly if they granted any public money directly or indirectly to institutions that do not provide a complete financial accounting to their own members or to public authorities." I also noted that the National Association of (Catholic) laity, composed of some twenty affiliated Catholic lay groups, had called for a moratorium on Catholic school construction in each diocese until the "existing crisis in all areas of Catholic education" is studied by "an independent research agency."

The crisis in Catholic education was not simply the shortage of teaching nuns or the unwillingness of the bishops to ask Catholics to support parochial schools, but a structural problem of morale described by the Jesuit weekly, *America,* in March 1966: "Without formal budgets, adequate accounting and cost analysis and annual financial reports, we do not really know what Catholic education is costing the Catholic community. It is time that we did know and that we organize our schools so that we shall know."

As the debate drew to a close, Fr. Blum got angry and attacked me, charging that I was opposed to children. I replied that he was interested only in Catholic children and challenged him to abandon aid to Catholic schools and join me in "adopting the Canadian family allowance program wherein payments are made to each family regardless of the religion and income of the parents." I said, "If the state provides money for children, let it provide for all, and not be a religious tax designed to aid two or three sectarian school systems. Let any grant to the rich be siphoned off in graduated income taxes. Let the Methodist and the Baptist and the atheist child have his grant as well as the Roman Catholic and Christian Reformed, the pre-school child as well as the school child."

It was obvious from the audience reaction that Blum had lost the debate when he rejected my challenge and was perceived as narrowly sectarian in his concern for children.

The debates in Michigan and the organization by opponents of parochiaid paid off a year later when a proposed Michigan Constitutional Amendment to prohibit public aid to non-public schools, except for transportation, was put on the November 1970 ballot. It was known as "Proposal C." Proposal C was planned to nullify a law adopted by the state legislature which would pay lay teachers in private or parochial schools. That law had been supported by the state Chamber of Commerce.

Proposal C was not expected to pass because the State Board of Education; the Missouri Synod Lutheran and Christian Reformed Church leaders; Cardinal Dearden; Henry Ford II; the president of General Motors; AFL, CIO and UAW leaders, and various industrialists and bank presidents opposed it.

However, when the vote was taken, Proposal C was adopted by a substantial majority. The people of Michigan saw clearly that approval of Proposal C helped restore the wall of separation of church and state.

Meanwhile, a quite different threat to that separation was advanced by the Creation Research Society, which advocated the teaching of creationism in Missouri public schools as an alternative scientific theory to evolution. I appeared before the Missouri House Education Committee February 17, 1989, on behalf of the ACLU of Western Missouri and the Jewish Community Relations Bureau of Greater Kansas City. I opposed the "creation science" bill for several reasons:

1) "This legislature did not mandate the teaching of evolution. It ought not to mandate the teaching of creationism. It is the proper function of a legislature to decide that courses should be taught in such subjects as history, English, foreign languages and science. It is not the function of a legislative body to write the science curriculum or to tell teachers how to teach it.

2) "This bill promotes sectarian religion under the guise of scientific theory. The teaching of creation is dependent on two faith assumptions: a) that a deity exists external to the universe, and b) that He created the universe, earth and all living things by suspension of natural laws. These faith assumptions cannot be reduced to scientific theory for two reasons: a) There is no way to verify them by scientific observation or testing and b) those who want creationism taught would not abandon it on the basis of any scientific data to the contrary, because for them it is faith."

I cited various other reasons for defeating the bill, including constitutional ones, and noted that "it seems prejudicial and obviously non-scientific to assert that God made 'life from nothing (definition of creation)' but that there could be no 'emergence of life from non-life' (definition of evolution).'"

The bill was defeated in committee. Nevertheless, a year later the creationists tried again with a bill purporting to guarantee academic freedom to teachers "who shall have the right . . . to present or cause to be presented any and all scientific evidence and knowledge" that supports creationism. When I appeared before the House Committee on Education February 16, 1980, on behalf of the ACLU of Eastern and Western Missouri, I presented numerous arguments but began with this: "This bill gives the teacher authority to determine what is scientific, without any review by school authorities and without reference to scientific method or the data of the scientific community." Moreover, "this bill could guarantee the tenure of incompetent teachers by making it impossible to dismiss for incompetency. A non-tenured teacher can make a *prima facie* case that his/her dismissal was because of belief and teaching about creation." The bill would also introduce religious controversy into the school system and violate the establishment clause of the First Amendment.

Others of course opposed the bill and it was killed in committee.

Although I testified on many occasions before Congressional committees, one testimony in February 1984 is particularly noteworthy, as it dealt with the U.S. establishment of diplomatic relations with the "Holy See," which is another name for the Papacy as a religious institution. I testified for the National ACLU because the ACLU Washington office staff refused to act on the matter. In fact, I took the issue to the 80-member national board, which by a nearly unanimous vote opposed the establishment of diplomatic relations. There were numerous other opponents, ranging from the Southern Baptist Convention to the National Council of Churches and Americans for Religious Liberty, all of whom opposed recognition on Establishment Clause grounds. The brunt of my testimony, however, was that it interfered with the free exercise of religion by Catholics in this country. In my introduction I noted that "it gives one church preferential status and hence changes the principle that all religious bodies in the U.S. have the same status and rights before the government."

In addition I said, "The construction of an embassy building, staffing salaries and travel to and from Rome comes out of tax money and represents a yearly subsidy for consultations with one religious body." My major point, which no one else advanced, was this: "It is a violation of the free exercise of religion by American Catholics in that an ambassador to the Pope will permit the President regularly to interfere with statements or actions by the Catholic bishops and priests who publicly differ with Administration policies. For example, President Reagan sent General Rowney to see the Pope on two occasions to curb the pastoral expression of the U.S. Catholic bishops in their Pastoral Letter on War and Peace which raised moral questions about the use of nuclear weapons. Unofficial but reliable reports indicate that the Pope did intervene with respect to that document along the lines of President Reagan's request." I cited reports in *The National Catholic Reporter,* January 20 and 27, 1984, as evidence.

At the conclusion of my testimony, Senator Jesse Helms, who was presiding, said he never expected to agree with any ACLU position as he did on this, and offered to hold up action for two weeks so that we could attempt to change the government's decision.

Not long thereafter I presented the same testimony before the U.S. Senate Appropriations Committee. Senator Warren Rudman was presiding in place of the chair, Senator Mark Hatfield, who was present. Senator Rudman interrupted my testimony and none of the others by saying the ACLU was an important organization and he wanted to ask me a question when I finished. This was his question: Suppose the U.S. is facing world domination by the Soviet Union and "the Pope tells all of his followers that it would be a sin to serve in the armed forces . . . do you mean to say that the U.S. Government at that point doesn't have a right through diplomatic means to try to convince the Holy See that they are jeopardizing this country and themselves? Do you mean that it is hands off as far as the ACLU is concerned?"

My response, in essence, was that the President of the United States can speak directly to the citizens of the U.S. instead of trying to influence their religious leaders "to change the minds of the church people." I said that "Roman Catholics in this country by and large do not accept judgments by the Vatican any more than Protestants accept judgments by their religious leaders instead of what each of them considers his or her conscience."

In addition I said, "It is both unethical and unconstitutional, and I think the President ought to be discouraged by the Senate from any such intervention in any church in this country."

When I finished my testimony I left the room immediately. Three portly gentlemen in clerical collars and black garments ran after me down the marble hall and thanked me for my testimony. They were Jesuit professors at Georgetown University. I asked them if someone representing the Catholic Church planned to testify. They responded vigorously, "We hope to God not!"

My defense of separation of church and state was not confined to legislative testimony, but included numerous periodical articles, chiefly for *The Nation; The Christian Herald;* a Methodist periodical, *The Christian Advocate; The Churchman;* The Humanist; and *The Christian Century.* Most of the time I submitted articles for publication, but in the case of *The Nation* the editor, Carey McWilliams, would phone and ask for a manuscript, as he knew I kept up with all facets of the issues of church and state.

Chapter 4
Abortion, Birth Control, and Population Politics

Abortion is a church-state issue because the Vatican insists that governments adopt into law its politics on birth control and abortion. I did not realize how serious this problem would become when I did the research and writing of a chapter on Civil Liberties and Abortion for the 1971 publication of the Methodist Board of Social Concerns, *Abortion, A Human Choice.* However, after the 1973 Supreme Court decision in *Roe v. Wade,* removing abortion from the criminal code, the Catholic bishops challenged the traditional American position that a person legally exists at birth (which is also the Biblical position) and insisted upon their theological position that an embryo or fetus from the moment of conception must have due process of law and equal protection with all living persons.

The basis for this proposal to amend the U.S. Constitution is the decision of Pope Pius XII on October 29, 1951: "Now the child, even the unborn child, is a human being in the same degree and by the same title as its mother . . . So . . . to save the life of the mother is a most noble end, but the direct killing of the [unborn] child as a means to that end is not lawful." This means that it is better for both mother and fetus to die than it is to save the life of the mother through a direct abortion.

In fact, Father Patrick A. Finney specifically said this in his book, *Moral Problems in Hospital Practices,* which was published under the imprimatur of the Archbishop of St. Louis: "Q. If it is morally certain that a pregnant mother and her unborn child will both die if the pregnancy is allowed to take its course, but at the same time the attending physician is morally certain that he can save the mother's life by removing the inviable fetus, it is lawful for him to do so? A. No, it is not. Such a removal would be a direct abortion."

In order to put Vatican directives into U.S. law, the Catholic bishops on November 20, 1975, issued their Pastoral Plan for Pro-Life Activities. It was clearly a political document. The Plan

43

stated, "It is absolutely necessary to encourage the development in each congressional district of an identifiable, tightly knit and well-organized pro-life unit." The Bishops also decided to "urge appointment of judges" who would take the Vatican position on abortion. The Plan listed specific directives for dealing with members of Congress and for legislative committees, such as "Contact members of the House Judiciary Subcommittee and get a commitment from each member." It also had a plan for Catholic high school seniors, for initiating contacts with non-Catholic churches and scholars. In short, the Catholic bishops have had a strategy since 1975 to persuade everyone to accept Papal decrees.

I saw this as having at least four implications. Here was the largest church in America, a tax-exempt organization whose leaders, accountable only to the Vatican, were clearly violating a fundamental American principle of separation of church and state. They were also prepared to subordinate the women of America to fetal life so that women were not only defined by the fetus but, once impregnated, whether by rape, incest or otherwise, their pregnancy was compulsory until birth.

Third, the bishops' decision to ban abortion was extended to contraceptive birth control and to preventing any further research on birth control devices even for the use of non-Catholics. And finally, the bishops intended to control the foreign policy of the United States so that no funding of family planning in other nations would take place and that the U.S. policy should be subject to Vatican approval. This is actually what happened during the Reagan and Bush presidencies.

As a result of this analysis I spoke at women's rallies in St. Louis, Louisville, Tulsa, Amarillo, Topeka and other cities around the country. I spoke in churches and universities from Dallas to Sacramento as well as across the midwest. The most significant meeting was a debate with one of the leading right-wing evangelists, D. James Kennedy, in Ft. Lauderdale, Florida on May 10, 1984 at an "Action for Life" Conference before a thousand hostile anti-choice activists.

Those present, with few exceptions, were right wing on other issues as well. In fact, a group of young right wing Catholic leaders, following the Bishops' Pastoral Letter in 1975, began persuading Protestant fundamentalist leaders to accept Vatican teaching on abortion as the centerpiece of their ministry. Paul Weyrich, a Catholic and founder of both the ultraright Free Congress Fundation and the Heritage Foundation, was the key figure in persuading Jerry Falwell to form the Moral Majority.[3] He also persuaded Pat Robertson to move into politics on this issue. James Kennedy is also a part of the inner circle, along with Weyrich, who meet to determine far right strategy not only on abortion but other issues.[4]

It was obvious that I was invited merely as a foil, so that the videotape would show Kennedy trouncing a pro-choice theologian. I refused to go on their terms of a ten-minute speech, and insisted on twenty minutes plus twelve-minute rebuttal, audience questions, and a neutral chairman as well as certain other requirements. They never used the videotape, and would not furnish me with a copy. It may even have been the only time Kennedy participated in a debate on any subject.

In his opening remarks, Kennedy, a Presbyterian or Calvinist by background, claimed that a fetus is a person recognized by God because in the Bible God called Isaiah and Jeremiah "in the womb." However, in Isaiah 49:1 the English translation (Revised Standard Version) says "God called me from the womb." In my response I said the Hebrew word "min" used in this passage is translated either "in" or "from," usually "from," and refers to a vocational calling from the earliest moment of birth. I also said that John Calvin, the greatest exegete of all time, referred to it as a vocational call, and until the anti-abortion movement began claiming that a fetus is a person, no one had used it for that purpose. In the question period one of Kennedy's followers asked if it was true that the word "min" could be translated either "in" or "from" the womb. Kennedy reluctantly admitted that I was correct. Again and again Kennedy failed either to maintain his position or to meet my arguments.

I wrote scores of articles for publication, some for *Christian Social Action,* some for *The Churchman,* but the most interesting one

---

[3] Both Connie Page in *The Right to Lifers* and Richard Viguerie in *The New Right* document this.

[4] Institute for First Amendment Studies, P.O. Box 589, Great Barrington, MA.

was published by the Sisters of Loretto, a progressive Catholic order, in their October 1990 newsletter, *CouRAGE*. The title the editor gave it was "Abortion: A Non-Violent Choice." It stated numerous ways in which women were subjected to violence if they did not have the choice of abortion.

For example, after noting that overt violence against women exists in such acts as rape (including spousal rape), incest and the Vatican's idea that a woman must remain pregnant because of a failed contraceptive, I said, "There is violence also in the idea embodied in some legislation that a woman may have an abortion only if the pregnancy endangers her life. This means that any damage to a woman's health short of death is 'acceptable' violence; suffering brought on by exacerbation of existing health problems such as diabetes or heart disease, and the shortening of her life thereby, are 'acceptable violence.'"

In early 1992 Stephen D. Mumford, who had seen a number of my articles, sent me a recently declassified government document, "National Security Studies Memorandum 200" (NSSM 200). Mumford, with a Master's degree in public health and a doctorate in population studies, is the director of the Center for Research on Population and Security. NSSM 200 is a 1975 "study of the impact of world population growth on U.S. security and overseas interests" by representatives of the U.S. Departments of Defense, Agriculture, State, the CIA and the Agency for International Development (AID). That major study was read and approved by President Richard M. Nixon and Gerlad R. Ford, and signed by Henry Kissinger and Brent Scowcroft.

It was mysteriously put under classification, presumed by Mumford to be the result of pressure from the Catholic bishops, since both Nixon and Ford felt it necessary to get Catholic support in their political campaigns. After reading NSSM 200, I discovered that one of its major warnings was against population wars, mass hunger, and other problems caused by overpopulation, many of them a potential threat to U.S. and world security. In it was the statement, "No country has reduced its population growth without resorting to abortion."

About the same time as I read NSSM 200, *Time* magazine of February 24, 1992, carried an important article entitled, "The U.S. and the Vatican on Birth Control," which began with this sentence:

"In response to concerns of the Vatican, the Reagan administration agreed to alter its foreign aid program to comply with the church's teaching on birth control." The article detailed various meetings between key administration Catholics and Pio Laghi, the Vatican's representative in Washington, as well as between State Department representatives who went to Rome to meet with officials of the Pontifical Council for the Family.

As a result of these disclosures and my own research about Vatican influence on U.S. legislation to support Vatican policy on birth control, I decided to convene a small group of leading American experts on population. In my capacity as president of Americans for Religious Liberty, I invited Stephen Mumford; R.T. Ravenholt, M.D., who had been the director of the State Department's Office of Population 1966-1979; Adolph W. Schmidt, President Nixon's Ambassador to Canada, and a few others to meet in Washington in May 14, 1992, with Edd Doerr, the director of Americans for Religious Liberty, and myself. We encouraged Mumford to write a commentary on NSSM 200 together with the full story of Vatican efforts to prevent national as well as international family planning. In 1995 Dr. Mumford sent me a pre-publication copy of *The Life and Death of NSSM 200,* a fascinating study of how Catholic bishops have been able to defeat a U.S. population policy.[5]

Even before Mumford's documented study I had published excerpts from a Seattle address by Dr. Ravenholt describing a meeting of Catholic bishops with Jimmy Carter during his campaign for the presidency. According to Ravenholt, the bishops agreed not to oppose Carter in return for his appointment of a leading Catholic who would dismiss Ravenholt and suspend international family planning by the U.S.

The year 1992 was also a critical time in the life of the United Methodist Church. The church's General Conference met in May in Louisville, Kentucky. The crucial issue was abortion. A strong right-wing movement called The Good News organization had arisen within the church, in part influenced by the Institute on Religion and

---

[5] *The Life and Death of NSSM 200: How the Destruction of Political Will Doomed a U.S. Population Policy* is available from the Center for Research on Population and Security, P.O. Box 13067, Research Triangle Park, NC 27709, 579 pp., $32.00 paperback, $39.00 hardcover.

Democracy, a right-wing pressure group, and in part indirectly by Catholic ideology transmuted through Jerry Falwell's Moral Majority and other right wing groups. Its major strength was in the South. However, it had some influence and its technique of attacking official church agencies made it seem to some agency leaders wise to stay neutral.

When I learned that not even the Board of Church and Society intended to defend abortion rights, I sent four mailings to over nine hundred General Conference delegates spaced three weeks apart. The first was a theological-Biblical defense of a woman's right to choose, which I wrote, entitled "Human Beings in the Image of God." The second was the Sisters of Loretto newsletter with my article "Abortion: A Non-Violent Choice." The third analyzed the so-called "Durham Declaration," circulated by some clergy connected with the Duke University Divinity School in Durham, NC.

Among the headings of paragraphs of my "Durham" analysis are these: "Fetal biology not the image of God" and "Is Abortion a litmus test required for salvation?" Since the Durham group condemned those who spoke of unwanted children and instead said "Children in the womb" are "gifts from God," I asked, "Is a fetus without a brain or heart a gift from God? Or a child with Tay-Sachs disease who will die an early and painful death? Or a pregnancy that will seriously endanger a woman's life or health a gift of God?" Then I urged Methodists to "examine carefully the false use of theological rhetoric to describe as 'gifts of God' any and every outcome of pregnancy "as if God is not only uncaring but a sexual determinist who thinks the result of any intercourse is God's gift which must be carried to term."

The fourth analysis was of a North Georgia Conference proposal that sought to change the phrase "birth control" to "conception control." It paralleled the Catholic theory of "a moment of conception" and advocated adoption instead of abortion. They held up Sarah and Hannah as Biblical models of women who nurtured children to whom they did not give birth. Evidently they had not recently read those passages because Sarah drove Ishmael into the desert and Hannah also was not a good example as there was no evidence she nurtured the children of her husband's other wife. Instead she "wept and would not eat" and "was sorely troubled" until she gave birth to Samuel.

Then I went to General Conference, although not a delegate, and briefed colleagues in the legislative committee considering abortion. On the only one of a number of motions that the anti-abortionists succeeded in adopting I wrote the minority report which prevailed on the General Conference plenary session, along with the motion that upheld the right of women to choose.

Again in the 1996 General Conference in Denver, which I attended, I briefed key members of the legislative committee on abortion and organized some informal lobbying. The moderates present sustained previous General Conference resolutions.

The lessons from these encounters is clear. The movement set in motion by the Vatican and the Roman Catholic bishops has expanded to right wing groups in the Protestant churches. The Southern Baptist Convention, in a turn away from its long tradition of support for "soul liberty," has adopted essentially a Catholic rationale for opposing separation of church and state, abortion, and favoring aid to parochial schools. In spite of the fundamentalist take-over of the Southern Baptists and a large segment of the Republican Party, the mainline Protestant churches have not succumbed to Vatican decrees. And even about 1,500 Southern Baptist congregations, frequently called moderates, have formed their own Fellowship and maintain a position of separation of church and state.

In addition to these actions I have had published at least fifteen articles in periodicals with respect to the importance of legal abortion and the right to choose, many of them in *The Churchman* (later known as *The Human Quest*), edited by Edna Ruth Johnson.

My most significant essay appeared in the *St. Louis University Public Law Review* (Vol. XIII, No. 1, 1993) entitled "Abortion and Public Policy," subsequently republished by Americans for Religious Liberty together with an *amicus* brief of 167 distinguished scientists and physicians to the Supreme Court that dealt with the questions of when human life begins, the time of viability, and the timetable of brain development.[6]

It is clear from the published statements of leading Catholic figures that some in the American Catholic hierarchy view the struggle to end abortion in the United States as crucial, not only to

---

[6] Available from Americans for Religious Liberty, P.O. Box 6656, Silver Spring, MD 20916, for $10.00.

Vatican authority over Catholic women, but over governments, an authority that has steadily eroded in most European countries and is now being fought out in the United States. The clearest statement was Cardinal John O'Connor's made at the Franciscan University of Steubenville in Ohio on April 3, 1992, when he said, "The fact is that attacks on the Catholic Church's stance on abortion -- unless they are rebutted -- effectively erode Church authority on all matters, indeed on the authority of God himself." He also said "Abortion has become the number one challenge for the Church in the United States because . . . if the Church's authority is rejected on such a crucial question as [the Catholic dogma about] human life . . . then questioning of the Trinity becomes child's play, as does the questioning of the divinity of Christ or any other Church teaching." This is obviously an overstatement, as there is much more depth to Catholicism than the papal positions on abortion and birth control or even the question of papal infallibility and authority. Many religions in the world thrive under creative, democratic leadership rather than under authoritarian control.

It is obvious that if Americans want to maintain separation of church and state and not succumb to pressures from the Vatican and fundamentalist Protestants on Congress and state legislatures, abortion must remain legal. If right wing religious leaders cannot persuade their own women members to refrain from abortion they ought not to be able to use the police power of the state to enforce punishment for what they regard as sin.

One of the most important organizations in the fight for legal abortion is Catholics for a Free Choice, with which I have been happy to cooperate. Their July, 1996, report of various public opinion polls indicates that 82% of U.S. Catholics say abortion should be legal under certain circumstances or without restrictions; that only 13% say abortion never can be a morally acceptable choice, and 70% say Catholics can vote in good conscience for candidates who support legal abortion.

What this means is that most Catholics are not prepared to accept the hard position of the Vatican that its position must become law for all Americans. So the issue for them as for most Americans is that of not allowing right wing spokesmen to breach the wall of separation between church and state, but one of upholding the right of women of all faiths or none to choose.

Chapter 5
Threats from the 1960s Far Right

When we moved to Kansas City in June of 1960 from New York, the contrast was amazing. Kansas City was a quiet, conservative, non-cosmopolitan place. There were no demonstrations, no radical movements, no anti-war activity, and few whites who were prepared to be involved in directly opposing racial discrimination and segregation. My own involvement with blacks, the anti-war movement, and civil liberties efforts soon led to newspaper reports and media interviews. In turn this produced right-wing reaction.

A man named Wayne Morse (not related to the distinguished U.S. senator from Oregon) became an implacable adversary of mine, picketing my meetings and otherwise working against me. He labeled himself an "Americanist," or one "who believes in a pure America -- a country which should be all-white, all Christian, and all-for-all, without any international ties with 'traitor' nations and without any 'left-wingers and liberals.'" (Kansas City *Town Squire,* January 1973)

We first confronted each other when Martin Luther King came to Kansas City to speak at the Municipal Auditorium on November 4, 1962. It was the traditional Reformation Day Service and the clergy were robed, ready to begin their processional. Morse was parading up and down outside with a sign that said: "Martin Luther King is a Commie Lover." I decided to counter-picket him and improvised a sign which said: "I love this racist Morse even though he and the Commies oppose equality." When King, whom I knew from F.O.R. days, heard of this he delayed the processional long enough to come out and greet me. Thereafter, my public meetings received Morse's attention. His picketing sign now was "John M. Swomley, Jr. is a Commie Lover."

Eventually we received harassing anonymous phone calls with the phone ringing frequently and various voices heard. I suspected Wayne Morse was the originator of these calls, but could not prove it. He would call me from time to time to express his disagreement with my positions, but would always identify himself. One day, knowing that he agreed with me on one issue, separation of church and state, I told him when he called that I was preparing testimony for a Missouri legislative committee against aid to parochial schools, but couldn't complete it because of so many harassing phone calls, some even interfering with our sleep. Without thinking, he blurted out: "Oh, I didn't realize that. We'll stop them."

They were stopped temporarily, but subsequently increased, and by 1964 we were receiving threatening calls at night. We would be wakened about 2 a.m. and again about 3 a.m. with this message: "We've got the cross-hairs on the back of your neck sighted, Swomley. God damn you, we're going to get you!" These calls sounded like those of the Minute Men, whose leader, Robert DePugh, and headquarters were at nearby Norborne, Mo. There were also Minute Men in Kansas City.

In the meantime, after a sermon I preached in the summer of 1963 at the Trinity Evangelical United Brethren Church in Kansas City, a man named Hubert Johnson, Chief of Racial Intelligence for the F.B.I. in Greater Kansas City, identified himself to me. My sermon was on "Nonviolence in Race Relations." He said, "I liked that sermon. Here is my card with my office and home phones. Call me day or night if you are in trouble." In spite of my relationship with William C. Sullivan of the F.B.I., outlined in a separate chapter, I continued my long-time suspicion of the F.B.I. and did not phone him. However, he phoned me often to ask interpretation of ideology and racial events in Kansas City or to inquire what I was doing.

One evening in April, 1964, Johnson phoned our house. I recognized his voice though he did not this time identify himself by name. He said simply: "The F.B.I. has infiltrated certain extremist organizations. If I were you I would not enter any lighted room in your house at night without first pulling the shades." I told him that I had a phone message that evening from a Jerry Brooks, whom I suspected was a Minute Man; that Brooks had offered to give me certain documents being circulated about me if I would meet him at an address in the inner city. Johnson said, "I hope you're too smart to go," and hung up his phone. I followed his advice. Since nothing I did or planned to do was secret and since all of the nonviolent activities in Kansas City were openly acknowledged, I had no hesitation in answering Johnson's inquiries about them. When he retired he actually asked me if I would be an FBI informant. I immediately and totally rejected that and never had another call from anyone in the FBI about anything.

Among my activities that antagonized the right wing in Kansas City were my frequent participation in interracial actions, including defense of blacks, and my participation in a radio broadcast with two top members of the Communist Party. The broadcast was a four-hour radio debate over station KBEA on January 10, 1964, with Gus Hall, the leader of the American Communist Party, and Arnold Johnson, in charge of education and public relations for the Communist Party, against Kenneth Goff, national director of Soldiers of the Cross, an extreme right-wing group. The producer of the program told me that Goff, then on the extreme right, was an ex-Communist and he needed two people, myself and another, who had never been Communists, so I persuaded Boyd Mather, a professor of mathematics at the University of Missouri, to participate.

It was an unusual event in suburban Kansas City, where the station was located. About twenty police and sheriff's deputies were there with rifles, some on rooftops surrounding the station. Wayne Morse was there with his signs. There were numerous call-ins during the program. I was accused of being pro-Communist by the extreme right, because they feel they are the only true anti-Communists. In general there was an assumption that the Communists were devils, and the only question from the radio audience was whether the position of the extreme right or mine, which not only respected their civil liberties but their personality as human beings, was correct. The next morning the *Kansas City Times* gave two columns to describing and quoting Gus Hall, and simply listed me with others as also "on the program," without any indication that we were opponents in a debate. Roy Carney lost his job at KBEA for producing the program.

On Sunday, April 6 the same year, 1964, I was scheduled to preach at a large black church, Centennial United Methodist. On April 4 my wife received threatening calls warning me not to appear at the church. When I returned April 5 from an out-of-town speaking engagement, I received similar calls. Early Sunday morning the police called to ask if I wanted a police escort. They had received bomb threats and were searching the building. I declined the police escort and urged them not to appear. The police captain told me politely that whether I wanted it or not, there would be an unmarked police car at each of the four corners of the block where the church was located and armed plainclothes officers inside the church.

My wife and I decided to go to the church and put our two small children in the nursery with the other children. I drove around the church and spotted the four police cars, each with two officers inside. Wayne Morse was there picketing and I invited him to come inside to the service. Morse told me later that when he entered the church, a big black detective put his hands on the lapels of Morse's coat and threatened bodily harm to him if he so much as opened his mouth in the church. My sermon was not very good, but the atmosphere was electric. However, nothing happened.

In 1964 I joined Charles Blackmar, a prominent Republican lawyer (now on the Missouri Supreme Court); Professor Norman Royall of the University of Missouri; Howard F. Sachs, an attorney (later a Federal District Court Judge); Robert Olsen and Irving Achtenberg, both attorneys, and others, in forming the Greater Kansas City Council for Responsible Dialogue. It was our attempt to combat extremism with open discussion of the issues. Blackmar was president and I was secretary. In spite of our efforts the extremism, including my harassing phone calls, continued into 1967.

In February 1967 Wayne Morse was convicted of assaulting a black female elevator operator in City Hall, and was sentenced to sixty days in the Municipal Farm. Midway in his jail term I decided to visit him. I was unannounced, and he was shocked as he descended the stairs into the visiting room on February 22. On the top stair, when he saw me, he said, "My God! Swomley!" Nevertheless we talked. In the course of our conversation I asked him if his wife needed money for shopping while he was in jail, and offered to lend her some. Sternly he told me he wanted no help from Swomley. Then I asked if she drove a car and he said she did not. I offered to drive her to the supermarket. Again he rejected any help from me. Later, I discovered that I was the only person who visited him in jail.

When his sentence was over he had changed his attitude toward me. I was no longer his enemy. The picketing of my meetings stopped. Soon he began to phone me simply to converse or to ask my opinion or to inform me of what he was doing. There was no ideological change and he continued to picket and harass others.

In the meantime, Robert DePugh, the leader of the Minutemen, had been indicted and convicted in 1967 for violations of the National Firearms Act. DePugh, who was head of Biolab Laboratories in Norborne, Missouri, told a *Kansas City Star* reporter in 1964 of his interest in bacteriological warfare. "Do you realize," he said, "that I could kill everyone in the United States except myself, if I wanted to?" He explained that by taking viruses from his laboratory, immunizing himself over a period of two weeks, and infecting or coughing on enough outbound passengers at the Kansas City air terminal he could wipe out the nation (*Kansas City Star,* August 18, 1964).

DePugh indicated that thousands of Minutemen had joined the National Rifle Association, that they had organized or joined gun clubs. He also was reputed to have assassination lists. A *Kansas City Star* reporter, J. Harry Jones, interviewed DePugh just after his conviction to ask what he planned to do while his case was on appeal and before he went to jail. DePugh said he had an assassination list. His list was headed by Senator J. William Fulbright. Harry Jones then said, "These are all national figures. Do you have a local list?" He did, and my name headed that list.

Harry Jones phoned our house and described for my wife the conversation with DePugh. I was in Washington, D.C. speaking when my wife phoned me. I did two things immediately. I phoned the dean of Saint Paul, E. Dale Dunlap, who lived about three blocks from us, to ask him to lift the hood of our car each morning until I returned to see if there was anything unusual there like a bomb, so that my wife would not be injured. I also asked another colleague, Bruce Rahtjen, to phone Wayne Morse, an acknowledged friend of DePugh, to tell him I was out of town for a week.

When I returned to Kansas City I wrote DePugh a letter telling him I thought he sincerely wanted to defend the United States by his methods, and that I wanted to defend the Constitution by mine. My method was to defend the Bill of Rights, including the right to free speech. Since I doubted if he had spoken from a public platform since his indictment, I invited him to speak at a student assembly at our school. He did not answer that letter or several follow-up invitations. Soon after my visit to Wayne Morse in jail, and after his hostility had ceased, I appealed to Morse to speak to DePugh and endorse my invitation. Morse did, and DePugh wrote me, agreeing to speak. Then I had second thoughts about such a speech, and proposed that I interview him with questions I would submit in advance. He agreed.

On April 26, 1967, DePugh arrived early at Saint Paul School of Theology. We met for the first time, and he told me he had just read my book, *The Military Establishment,* and to his surprise found himself in substantial agreement with much of it since it was critical of the military and American foreign policy. The Assembly had the best attendance in the school's history. However, DePugh was courteously treated; students were attentive and asked him serious questions. Some time later Wayne Morse told me that he asked DePugh whether he was surprised at the treatment in the school and "at the hands of that man." He admitted he was.

Then I began sending DePugh a newsletter on international affairs called *Current Issues,* which I wrote each week and which the Fellowship of Reconciliation sent to about a thousand people in the U.S. and around the world. I asked DePugh for his criticisms. He wrote penned comments in the margins and returned them to me. The last one I received before he went underground to avoid prison included this comment on my term "imperialism," which he had circled: "I think many people would find this idea more palatable if you could find a different word -- 'imperialism' is so often thought of as a Communist 'catchword.'" With comments such as that it became evident that he no longer viewed me as an enemy or a Communist.

Two of the three counts of National Firearms Act violations on which DePugh had been convicted in November 1966 had been dismissed by the Court of Appeals, and a retrial was ordered on the remaining count. On February 20, 1968, DePugh was indicted by a federal grand jury on a charge of bank robbery and conspiracy with respect to banks near Seattle, Washington, where F.B.I. agents had arrested seven Minutemen. DePugh went underground, and successfully eluded the F.B.I. for more than a year, all the time communicating with various people and reporters by written and phone messages.

Eventually DePugh was caught and sentenced to ten years in Federal prison. On April 21, 1972, I was in Atlanta for a meeting. That afternoon I spent three and a half hours visiting DePugh in the Federal prison. We discussed prison life, international affairs, Communism, and various other topics. Many months before that visit I had written DePugh and continued a chiefly political and intellectual correspondence. DePugh had some artistic talent, and gave me a painting he had done in prison, as well as a copy of a book he wrote there.

At the end of April of 1972, DePugh's mother phoned me to say she had sent legal briefs to the American Civil Liberties Union national office asking them to intervene on his behalf with an *amicus* brief to persuade the Supreme Court to grant *certiorari*. She asked me to phone A.C.L.U. I explained that any A.C.L.U. decision to intervene would be on the merits and not because a member of the National Board, as I was by then, had expressed an interest in the case. The A.C.L.U. declined intervention and the Supreme Court also refused *certiorari*.

Months later in early October 1972, DePugh's mother phoned to ask me if I would write a letter to the U.S. Board of Parole recommending his release on parole. For almost two weeks I "stewed" over this request, wondering whether I should encourage the release of a potentially dangerous man. Finally I wrote on October 13 to James R. Pace, the parole executive, describing my strong opposition to DePugh's political views, my conversations and correspondence with him, and then stated my reasons for parole. One of my five points follows:

Insofar as punishment or isolation from society is a deterrent to future violations of the law, ten years will not accomplish more than two or three.

Robert DePugh told me of his own reflections and work while in prison. He seems to be free from bitterness about society and hopeful about the future. Both of these are good signs. There is a point in anyone's existence in prison when hopelessness and bitterness enter the picture. The time for parole, it seems to me, is before that occurs.

I have no idea whether my letter was a factor or cause of DePugh's parole, but within about four months he received word of his parole. I wrote him a series of letters urging him to give up his gun or firearms activity and his political involvements and devote his time to being a good husband and father. In his letter of March 27, 1973, he wrote me: "34 days to go. Needless to say, I'm counting them one by one. I do intend to take your advice on political activity seriously and for the first time in several years, I expect to put the happiness and welfare of my own family first."

It is true that after my changed relationships with Wayne Morse and Robert DePugh I had no more threats against my life and no further harassing telephone calls. The right wing, however, continued not only to exist in Kansas City and in the U.S. but after some years to expand its influence nationally.

Nevertheless, the years of the Vietnam war and the large-scale nationwide increase in anti-war activity following the important civil rights victories of the sixties, changed the climate so that my association with minorities and my peace or anti-war activity never again drew the same kind of reaction locally.

Chapter 6
F.B.I.: Confidential

My experience with the Federal Bureau of Investigation has ranged from one of being investigated for sedition during World War II to that of a confidential relationship with a high-ranking F.B.I. official. The virtue of telling the story, aside from any historical interest, is the insight it may offer into the way a secret federal police agency operates inside a democracy.

The high-ranking official was William C. Sullivan, assistant director of the F.B.I., who was in charge of investigating and dealing with "subversive activities" including those of Communists, the Ku Klux Klan, the American Nazi Party, and of racial groups such as the Black Panthers. He was the only person J. Edgar Hoover, the authoritarian director, permitted to speak publicly for the Bureau, other than himself.

I first met Sullivan in 1961 at a luncheon in Greenwich, Connecticut, which included people from around the country who had met to discuss the growing threat of right-wing extremist activity, as evident, for example, in the John Birch Society. I had been asked to attend by Sidney Lawrence, the director of the Jewish Community Relations Bureau in Kansas City. We sat at one end of a long table. When Sullivan learned of my Methodist background, he explained that he was a devout Irish Catholic from Boston, but had always gone to Methodist schools and colleges, had received scholarships from them, and had a warm spot for Methodists. He invited me to let him know when I came to Washington so that we might have lunch together. He also suggested that we keep in touch by mail.

When I went to Washington about four or five times a year, traveling usually by train in those days, Sullivan would meet me at the Union Station, where we would talk for an hour or so before I went to my meeting. Or we would go to lunch. He insisted that everything he told me or wrote me was confidential, partly by its nature, and partly because of his fear of J. Edgar Hoover. On one occasion in a Union Station conversation I asked him why the F.B.I. did not investigate crime, but specialized in "subversive" activity. He said the F.B.I. ought to be investigating crime and the Mafia, but Hoover was not interested in that; he preferred to go after Communists and other "subversives."

Sullivan sent me copies of books, including one by Thomas Merton, another by Harry and Bonaro Overstreet, and especially those attributed to J. Edgar Hoover, with the implication that Sullivan had written or largely written them for Hoover. Sullivan also sent me copies of speeches after he delivered them, inviting my criticism and suggestions. These were chiefly on Communism, but also included lectures dealing with religion and other subjects. In his four-page letter of September 24, 1962, he said: "Your observations in the letter of August 9 were quite helpful and I have acted upon them." He also objected to some of my comments. For example: "You mentioned that I pointed out that prayer could be effective relative to overcoming Communism. You seem to object to this . . . . This coming from you, was a bit surprising because I was of the impression that you believed in all aspects of religion and their social application."

We discussed in our letters such things as the moral standards of Communists, peaceful coexistence, the inevitability of war, and were generally in disagreement. He wrote: "I know you will be disappointed, but I cannot accept all your reasoning in your thoughtful article on 'Communism and Co-existence.'"

On March 3, 1963, Sullivan wrote concerning his nomination for membership in the Cosmos Club of Washington: "I have taken the liberty of mentioning your name as one who would be willing to evaluate my academic qualifications for membership in the Cosmos Club, and make a recommendation one way or the other. I hope this is not troubling you too much." I wrote the letter.

So long as Sullivan sent me copies of his speeches, I sent him some of mine so that he would know of my radical non-violence position, my early opposition to the war in Vietnam, and my different analysis of the problems of Communism and of black power. I had for several years suspected that the reason he wanted to continue our relationship was the fact that I combined religion and politics, having a doctorate in political science as well as degrees in theology, the fact that I was a Protestant, and that my radical social analysis was a challenge to his position.

In 1968 and 1969 I wrote him several lengthy letters discussing black power and violence and Martin King's nonviolence. We also exchanged views on civil disobedience. In response to some of these letters he wrote me in May 1970: "Needless to say, in recent weeks I have thought of you more than once and of your philosophy of nonviolence. It is a very profound, practical and persuasive viewpoint. To actually work decisively nationwide, vast numbers would have to accept and act on this view . . . "

Frequently I challenged his positions. After one speech he made at a western university, I wrote on March 27, 1967: " . . . instead of recognizing that such movements as SDS (Students for a Democratic Society) have the cutting edge on the campus rather than the Dubois Clubs, you imply that SDS is really a tool of or simple collaborator, with the Communists. My own frequent contacts on college campuses reveal a different motivation. SDS's rationale for collaboration is non-political in the sense that they believe they should include everyone -- out of respect for personality. They are reacting to the exclusionism of the McCarthy days, etc. But they do not take their line from the Communists. If anything, the Communists are more conservative and less likely to be the leaders in the student left today."

In another letter, of July 15, 1968, I questioned some material he sent me which seemed to identify Black Power with violence. I wrote, "Black Power today as I understand it is at least this: an effort to give dignity to all black people by making them think black is beautiful -- intelligent -- powerful -- and that black people by working together can get enough power to be treated with justice and equality. Black people have their extremists, their moderates, their pacifists, etc. the same as whites. But it is the failure to recognize this, and to identify the term "Black Power" with violence that marks the identifier as basically racist."

However, our relationship involved more than correspondence or occasional conversations. On one occasion in January, 1969, while I was attending the annual meeting of the American Society of Christian Ethics at Wesley Theological Seminary in Washington, he called me out of the meeting to discuss an ethical problem relating to Martin Luther King. The F.B.I. had not only wiretapped King beginning in October 1963, with the consent of Attorney General Robert Kennedy, but on orders from Hoover had also kept him under constant surveillance.

As we sat in Sullivan's car in the parking lot, he told me that churches were beginning to put King's likeness in stained glass windows and that this troubled him greatly because of what he described as "sex orgies" in which King and other black Baptist pastors had participated. He had told me of this before but not in great detail. Moreover, it was with the assumption that this would not be made public. The question he asked me now was whether he should make public the F.B.I. record of King's sex life. My earlier reaction was one of suspicion about the F.B.I. evidence, and now of horror at this thought of making it public. But I said, "The trouble with you Catholics is that you have too many hangups about sex!" This did not help the conversation.

At one point, however, I turned to the question of privacy and confidentiality. I told him of a conversation I had had with Clarence Kelley, Chief of the Kansas City Police Department, on April 19, 1968, shortly after the Kansas City riots after King's murder. That police department and Kelley had been severely criticized by leading Protestant clergy as well as black leaders for the racism and brutality in the handling of the riot. Kelley announced to the press that he would not see or talk with any black leader or clergyman until he had completed his investigation. But in the course of a long but friendly adversarial relationship, Kelley had told me that anytime I wanted to see him he would arrange it. I phoned him, and after some hesitation he arranged an appointment for fifteen minutes which in fact lasted over an hour. We discussed the riot, Kelley's personal hurt, his real feelings, and his desire to be fair. I had proposed a procedure for his meeting with clergy and black leaders as a part of his investigation, because attitudes are as important as facts. The procedure called for no response from Kelley, only listening and questioning. His own pastor would preside. Kelley agreed, but it was vetoed by the chairman of the Police Board, which supervised the Department. Moreover, I told Sullivan that if I were to have made public my conversation with Kelley it would have improved Kelley's public image in Kansas City at a time when it was very poor. I asked him if I should have done that. Kelley had not asked confidentiality on this or any other of numerous occasions when we talked.

Sullivan was decisive in his comment: "Your conversation with Kelley was confidential and as privileged as the confessional." Then I made the point that Sullivan's invasion of King's privacy, which did not eventuate in King's arrest, was also as confidential as the confessional; that it could have no other purpose than to smear the reputation of a great man. We discussed the fact that many of the world's greatest leaders, including kings, popes, and leading American statesmen, such as Benjamin Franklin and Thomas Jefferson, had had illicit sexual relationships, that King's private life should not affect our evaluation of his public contribution.

Sullivan seemed convinced by our conversation, which lasted long into the night. At that time he did not make the information public. Unlike Hoover, Sullivan believed in civil rights for blacks and had hired the first black agents of the F.B.I. However, the story of the wiretaps and surveillance became public in June, 1969, whether by order of Hoover or by a decision of Sullivan approved by Hoover, I do not know. I left for a sabbatical in Argentina about that time.

When I came to Washington Sullivan always offered to put an F.B.I. car at my disposal. I always refused, not only because it was a misuse of taxpayers' money but because I did not want to be beholden to the F.B.I.! Sullivan continued to try to be helpful, and this was a surprise when our family when to Buenos Aires for my sabbatical in July of 1969. I had not given our travel itinerary to him through Central and South America en route there, nor our address, which I did not know in advance. He did, however, know that I would be at the Facultad Evangelica de Teología in Buenos Aires. And only five minutes after we moved into the apartment we were allotted, the telephone rang. The voice on the other end said, "This is the F.B.I. in Argentina. Mr. Sullivan asked me to get in touch with you and be of any service to you while you are in Argentina." I thanked him for his courtesy, told him I could think of no reason for needing any service, but told him I would phone if I did.

Some weeks later my wife, who enjoys opera as I do, discovered that it was impossible to get tickets for any opera in the months ahead. They were sold out. Shortly thereafter the F.B.I. agent,

John Wachter, who served as legal attache at the U.S. Embassy, because by law the F.B.I. was not authorized to function overseas, phoned me again. In the course of the conversation I told him of our inability to get opera tickets. In a few days he phoned me to tell me that tickets would be available at the opera on a certain night. They were the best seats in the house -- a box above the stage.

Some days thereafter when I was in the section of Buenos Aires near the American Embassy, I stopped in his office to thank him. In the course of our conversation he asked me why I was in Argentina, what I wanted to accomplish and what some of my interests were. Among other things I mentioned an interest in Peronism and labor unions. There had been some general strikes against martial law while we were there. He excused himself, went to the other side of a huge office where there was another desk and telephone. It was too far away for me to hear any word of what was a fairly long conversation. When he returned he said, "I have been talking to the C.I.A. here. They have penetrated every labor organization in Argentina. I can arrange for you to visit any unions you want. But from what Mr. Sullivan told me about you, you might not want to work through the C.I.A." I told him Mr. Sullivan was correct, and that I would not take advantage of his offer.

On a few other occasions he phoned, but the only other personal contact occurred the day before we left. Mr. Wachter came to our apartment to say goodbye and to give us an Argentine painting he had purchased. We were planning to go from Buenos Aires to Brazil, where police state conditions existed, worse than martial law in Argentina. Since I had engaged in a demonstration in Buenos Aires, forbidden by law, he warned me of conditions in Brazil and gave me the day and night telephone numbers of the F.B.I. agent in Brazil in case I got in trouble. I never used those numbers.

I could understand Mr. Wachter's concern for me. William Sullivan was a stern disciplinarian. One of the agents in the Kansas City office told me that every agent stood in fear of him when he came to the office and that he expected obedience. Evidently Mr. Wachter very much wanted to please Sullivan.

My relations with Sullivan continued for a few years after our return from Argentina. In April 1970 he spoke at an assembly I had arranged at the Saint Paul School of Theology. There had been reports that the F.B.I. had infiltrated or was planning to infiltrate the

Methodist General Conference. A few faculty and students strongly criticized the F.B.I. for such infiltration and other illegal activity. Sullivan's hands were shaking as he responded, and denied that there had been or would be any infiltration of a church.

The last conversation I had with Sullivan was in a Chinese restaurant in Washington in October 1971, not far from a Methodist church where I was attending a meeting of the Methodist Board of Christian Social Concerns. Sullivan phoned to tell me that Hoover had locked him out of his office and that he was fired. He suggested that we have lunch together. At lunch he described some of his conflicts with Hoover. One was over the hiring of black agents. Hoover had said they weren't intelligent enough and had turned down all applications. Sullivan said that when two exceptionally able and intelligent blacks had applied he went to Hoover again. When Hoover said they couldn't pass the exam, Sullivan proposed that they be allowed to try "so we would know once and for all." Hoover grudgingly acquiesced; the two did well on their examinations, and Sullivan hired them. But Hoover was adamantly opposed when Sullivan proposed hiring female agents.

At one point Sullivan leaned across the table and asked me to make a guess as to how many card-carrying Communists there were in the United States. When I guessed 12,000, he said, "There are only 2,500, but Mr. Hoover wouldn't let us publicize that."

After that conversation our relationship ended except for a letter and one telephone conversation while he worked at the Federal Drug Enforcement Agency. Sullivan had had serious differences with Hoover for years, but usually kept these differences to himself. He was aware that no agent could disagree with Hoover and not be censured or fired. He tried to influence Hoover, sometimes with some success. Finally the rupture came. This is described in Sullivan's book, *The Bureau: My Thirty Years in Hoover's F.B.I.,* and need not be repeated here.

I had great respect for Sullivan. He was an unusual law enforcement officer, tough, demanding, principled, but with an open and questioning mind that led him into our relationship and, I understand, with others as well. When I sent for my F.B.I. record in 1976 under the Freedom of Information Act, there were 98 pages about my activities before I met Sullivan. There were none during the period of our relationship, and only a later letter about me written by Clarence Kelley during his tenure as Director of the F.B.I., based on his knowledge of me when he was Chief of Police in Kansas City, as alluded to earlier. Sullivan was constantly at work and under great pressure, yet he was apparently not too busy to keep my F.B.I. file clear. He was aware that I was involved in numerous activities that Hoover would have judged with suspicion. In one of my letters I urged Sullivan not to work so hard, but to take a vacation. I said: "Too bad you can't enjoy this cool Colorado air and get away for a brief vacation. It is our common recognition of sin that keeps both the F.B.I. and the clergy busy. But since there are more clergymen than F.B.I. agents, I can easily take a vacation and let my colleagues look after things for awhile. I hope you will be able to do the same before the summer is over."

Unfortunately, Sullivan was killed in a hunting accident. I know none of the details and none of the names of those in the hunting expedition, yet I have wondered if it was an accident. His death, however, released me from the confidentiality of our relationship, which he expected while working for J. Edgar Hoover and the F.B.I.

William Pepper's book, *Orders to Kill: The Truth Behind the Murder of Martin Luther King,* makes a strong case that the FBI, along with other agencies, was involved in the planning for King's assassination. When I had specifically asked Sullivan at the time if James Earl Ray was guilty, he told me evidence pointed to Ray. I assume he could not have told me the truth given his position in the FBI, and I cannot imagine that he did not know.

Chapter 7
Kansas City

When I came to Kansas City in July, 1960, to teach social ethics at Saint Paul School of Theology, I came with no social action agenda and was virtually a stranger to the city. Events soon involved me directly in the city's police and racial tensions. I joined two local organizations, both of which were new to Kansas City: the Greater Kansas City American Civil Liberties Union, and the Interfaith Committee for Civic Action, whose purpose was to make Kansas City government "representative of all the citizens" instead of the political bosses and factional groups which had long controlled the city. I was put on the committee to watch the police, and from time to time at night rode in squad cars.

I was soon convinced not only that the police did not impartially administer the law, but with some exceptions were very racist. One black detective, Leon Jordan, warned me early with friendly advice not to try to expose or investigate police connections with organized crime. By and large I took his advice because my experience and expertise led me in other directions. However, I was one of those who participated in a decision which was reported as follows in the March 17, 1961, *Kansas City Times:* "The Interfaith Committee for Civic Action endorsed legislation yesterday for a continuous county grand jury, offered support for a federal investigation of an alleged link between some political elements and the underworld," and sent a telegram to Robert F. Kennedy, Attorney General of the U.S., favoring a continuing investigation by the Justice Department of Kansas City's link with organized crime.

My first major project involving racial tensions came as a result of serving as guest minister for a few Sundays at Centennial Methodist Church, the largest black Methodist church in Kansas City, during the summer of 1961. A young man of nineteen, William H. (Butch) Hunter, who was a member of the church, had been arrested for the killing on August 28 of a white policeman, Corporal Arthur J. Marti. I visited Hunter in the Jackson County jail at the request of his parents and grandparents, and listened to his story.

Briefly, his account referred to some young black gangs warring against each other. Some of his friends in one gang, which had been threatened, pressured Hunter to bring them his grandfather's rifle and revolver. On Hunter's way to deliver the guns he was accompanied by four friends. An unmarked car driven by a white man in civilian clothes pulled up and told the boys to stop. Hunter threw the gun into some bushes. When the man pointed a gun at the boys and told them to place their hands on his car, Hunter removed the revolver from his pocket and bent over to put it under the car. The man, who had not identified himself as a police officer, demanded the gun.

Hunter handed the gun over, whereupon the officer, according to Hunter, "started hitting me over the head with the gun, across the forehead and across the face, approximately four or five times." Hunter tried to grab the gun and stop the beating, and in the process the gun went off and killed the officer. I believed Hunter, a very shy and mild-mannered youth, but decided to investigate by going into the block where the killing had taken place, and also interviewing the others who had been with Hunter. At first I got nowhere until I took a black minister, Cecil Williams, with me on successive nights. After all, I was white and unknown and could have been on the other side. Everyone I interviewed confirmed Hunter's version; but one black youth had fled the city out of fear of the police.

In the meantime Hunter's grandparents had hired a lawyer, R.B. Kirwan, who pocketed the $1,500 but did not seek any witnesses. When I reproached him, he said he could arrange a manslaughter conviction. Nonetheless I provided witnesses and tried to construct a case for the lawyer. Officer Marti had a long record of police brutality against Negroes, but this did not come up at the trial before an all-white jury. At the trial in December, 1961, Hunter reported being beaten by arresting officers. The prosecuting attorney, J. Arnot Hill, used racist language during the trial, some of which was ordered stricken by Judge McQueen.

The defense attorney did not ask for acquittal, but suggested manslaughter. Hill asked for the death penalty. During the trial I sat beside Gwendolyn Wells, a professor of law at the University of Kansas City, who told me that Hunter could not possibly have pulled the trigger, given the prosecutor's description of the encounter. The prosecutor himself suddenly recognized this, and did not continue his description. Nevertheless, the jury convicted Hunter of second degree murder, and he was sentenced to life in prison, entering the Missouri State Penitentiary January 26, 1962.

I continued to correspond with Hunter while he was in Missouri prisons, visited him, and appeared at his parole hearing along with a black former police sergeant, Alvin Brooks. Hunter worked as clerk in the Protestant chapel, directed the choir, and after taking dental technician courses, became supervisor of the dental laboratory. After his parole in August 1971, Hunter enrolled in Lincoln University, took a major in law enforcement, and subsequently was asked by the state parole board to become a parole officer.

A major racial incident occurred in April 1962 when Lorenzo Worten, a black man, purchased a house in an all-white housing project in Vineyard Woods. Fires were started in the Worten house, windows broken, and inside walls defaced. When I returned home from Washington, D.C., a colleague, Carl Bangs, called my attention to the news story on April 3. That afternoon I went to see the damaged property, talked to the owner and others. Then I started phoning ministers in Greater Kansas City. By 5 p.m. I had about thirty ministers committed to joining me that evening in calling on families in the neighborhood.

I phoned Chief of Police Clarence Kelley with whom I served on a Citizens Committee on Crime and Juvenile Delinquency. He seemed pleased to know of our project, and notified police in the area so they would know we were not troublemakers. I also phoned Robert Adams, Director of the Kansas City Human Relations Commission, and asked him to duplicate a report of the Laurenti Sociological Study which showed property values do not necessarily decrease when Negroes move in.

Adams and I briefed the ministers. My approach was to assume that the white neighbors were distressed and needed the therapy of having someone listen to their problem. We also offered to help them accept the situation and maintain their property values. Since some of the group were my students, I assigned a student to a practicing pastor and we went by twos for our calling. The fifteen teams called on approximately fifty families. I took the immediate neighbors on both sides of the street and discovered who had probably set the fires.

We received written reports on 37 of the families; of these 18 had a positive attitude, five were neutral, and four negative. Nine indicated they had no intention of moving, and one definitely planned to move. The next morning a front-page story in the *Kansas City Times* described our project. Chief of Police Kelley called the President of our theological school, Dr. Don Holter, and told him our action was worth ten squad cars patrolling the area.

An interracial group of persons, including Robert Hoyt, Lee Vertis Swinton, Julia Hill, Rev. A. Cecil Williams, and Robert Farnsworth went to the Worten house to set up a workshop to repair it. As soon as the family moved into the repaired house I asked the student body at our school for volunteers who would sit in the Worten home on a sofa in front of their large window in the front of the house. We were able to provide at least two students for two-hour stretches morning, afternoon and evening. A police car parked nearby at night. We told the hostile neighbors nothing, letting them assume, if they wanted, that these were plainclothes men inside. In fact, the students were studying and reading.

In the meantime, I had become actively involved in almost every level of the struggle to end racial injustice in Kansas City. In January 1962 I was invited to join a fourteen-member Committee to Study Crime and Delinquency in Kansas City. It was chaired by Dr. Earl Thomas, the black principal of Lincoln High School, a segregated black school, and later a member of the City Council; and included the new Chief of Police, Clarence Kelley, and the Superintendent of Schools, James Hazlett. In spite of serving on a committee with Chief Kelley, I was almost constantly involved in an adversarial confrontation with him over various cases of police brutality against black citizens, including some killings by the police.

These confrontations, some of which were as a representative of the local A.C.L.U., and some on my personal initiative, led Chief Kelley in late 1962 to appoint his highest-ranking officer, Lt. Col. Don Phillips, as the Police Department's Human Relations Officer. Soon after the appointment was made, I took Phillips to a meeting on February 18, 1963, of the Interdenominational Ministers Alliance, the organization of black ministers in Kansas City, of which I was a member as well. He listened for more than an hour as one member after another described personal experiences of humiliation or brutality at the hands of the police.

Dr. Don Holter, President of Saint Paul, and I conferred about the organization of a Kansas City Council on Religion and Race, and then called on Dean Lewis of the University of Kansas City Law School to ask if he would initially chair such a meeting. He agreed. Before long there was full participation by Catholic, Jewish, and Protestant agencies and a paid executive director at work.

In 1963 we organized a chapter of the Congress of Racial Equality, with Robert Farnsworth as chairperson. Apart from that, Rev. A. Cecil Williams, a black minister, and I organized the first major march in Kansas City of four hundred black citizens and a few whites, from the heart of the black area to the Kansas City Board of Education, to demand school integration.

This was the first occasion also when the police, under the leadership of Col. Phillips, cooperated fully with a black protest, stopping traffic at each intersection to permit the march to proceed.

I did not confine my efforts to protests, but had a conversation with Chief Kelley about the nature or composition of the police force. He indicated that it was difficult to recruit and train a non-racist police force, given the low salaries paid to police officers. As a result I began to enlist clergy and others in support of bills in the legislature for increased compensation and benefits for the police.

The next step, encouraged by various groups active in human relations in Kansas City, was a proposal for a City ordinance banning discrimination in places of public accommodation. I testified before a City Council Committee and engaged in public speaking on its behalf. In early 1964 I organized a Methodist Committee on Public Accommodation and secured the support of prominent newscasters, Bishop Eugene Frank, and others. As a result of the efforts of many, Kansas City became the first city of its size in the country to adopt by public vote a law forbidding discrimination in places of public accommodation such as barber shops and restaurants.

In late 1963 I was invited to become a member of the Research Academy, a group of black intellectuals who presented papers at monthly dinners and held extended discussions about the Kansas City racial scene. It was chaired by Dr. Girard Bryant, President of the

Metropolitan Community College, and included black school officials and other black civic leaders.

My social action in Kansas City was not limited to racial issues. Much of my spare time was spent working with the local A.C.L.U., defending civil and religious liberty in legislative hearings. I served as President of the Western Missouri and Greater Kansas City A.C.L.U. from 1969 to 1973, and therefore represented it before numerous public bodies both in Missouri and in Topeka, Kansas.

I helped Hugh Wamble organize Missouri Friends of the Public Schools in 1964, helped Sidney Lawrence and Charles Blackmar organize the Council for Responsible Dialogue to deal with right-wing extremism, and regularly attended a National Conference of Christians and Jews interfaith dialogue group.

I also maintained an active concern for working men and women, many of whom lived without adequate wages to maintain a decent standard of living. As a result, when the first walkout of Kansas City school teachers took place in October 1966, I was invited to address the members of the Kansas City Education Association. At that meeting I said that their action was "an appeal to the school board, but in another sense an appeal to the real estate board and the power structure. Your action is to trouble the conscience of men who have the welfare of the community at heart but who do not know what their actions are doing to you, to the schools and to their own children."

I went on to say that if a community does not pay the cost of improved education it will not attract industry, but it will pay for larger jails, more thefts and arson cases, and possibly even riots (*Kansas City Star,* October 3, 1966, p. 11).

I did not actually foresee that there would be a riot within the next seven months, or that in it $915,000 worth of property would be destroyed, scores wounded, and six persons left dead. The riot was triggered by the murder of Dr. Martin Luther King and by a school board decision, made in consultation with the police, to keep the schools in session instead of allowing students to demonstrate or otherwise mourn his death.

By chance I was teaching a course of more than twenty students in social action techniques. The students had chosen a project, "How to Prevent a Race Riot in Kansas City." Although I was out of town speaking when the riot occurred, my class members were involved night and day for several days in observing what happened and trying to assist people caught by police tear gas and shooting. I had a first-hand report of what happened when I returned. I wrote that story in detail, which was published in *Focus Midwest* (Vol. 62, No. 42). I also had a conversation with Chief of Police Kelley about it, and organized actions such as food supply to some black groups cut off from stores.

In 1970, after a series of violent incidents at universities because of the war in Vietnam, I was invited to be one of the speakers at a large anti-war rally at the University of Nebraska on May 9. There were about 7,000 present. The lead speaker's flight from Chicago was delayed, and the chairperson at the last minute asked for a volunteer among the other speakers to go first. I volunteered in order to set the tone of non-violence. In the preceding few days the R.O.T.C. building had been occupied and there were threats of burning it. I told students that if burned, it could be rebuilt; that it was better to urge students not to join R.O.T.C., because they could have R.O.T.C. without a building, but could not have it without cooperative students. Methodist Bishop James Armstrong, who was the next speaker, followed the same theme of non-violence, as did the other speakers. Two days later I spoke at a similar but smaller rally at the University of Missouri, Kansas City.

In 1978 when there was an anti-labor union "Right to Work" Amendment proposed for the Missouri Constitution, I went to the Central Labor Council office in Kansas City to volunteer to speak against it. At my first debate on the issue October 19 at Avila College, I learned that the only other person outside labor's ranks who volunteered to speak was Sister Pat Kenoyer, who was in the audience. The Amendment was subsequently defeated.

Several years later, Pat Kenoyer and I invited David Downing, a Disciples of Christ executive minister to join us on December 21, 1981, to plan the organization of the Greater Kansas City Interfaith Peace Council, now Interfaith Peace Alliance.

My peace activities were not confined to Kansas City. In 1981 I accepted an invitation by Japanese Buddhists to visit Japan in April 1981 with all expenses paid. The purpose was to participate in a World Assembly of Religious Workers for Peace. This was not only a significant meeting and introduction to Buddhist activism, but also an education about U.S. military institutions and activities in Japan.

There were twenty-six U.S. military bases, an irritating presence not only to Buddhists but to many others. In January 1982 some of the Buddhist leaders at the World Assembly visited Kansas City and participated in a march which I organized through the city center sponsored by the Kansas City Interfaith Peace Council.

In the summer of 1982 I wrote Sidney Lens, a Chicago peace and labor leader, and Daniel and Philip Berrigan, Catholic anti-war activists, to ask them to join me in a call to about fifty peace leaders to meet November 26 and 27 in Washington at the Institute for Policy Studies. About twenty-five came to the meeting. We tried unsuccessfully to unite the various peace groups around an "Agenda for Non-Collaboration" with nuclear war and deterrence.

In April 1983 I left Kansas City to fly to Nicaragua to join four other Americans and a delegation from the Dutch Inter-Church Peace Council, in Managua. We were one of the first if not the first delegation from the U.S. to tour war areas and meet with those favoring and opposing the Sandinista revolution. We also visited Honduras, from which the American Ambassador was directing the war against Nicaragua, and saw camps which housed contra families and guerrillas on rest leave. When I returned I visited the Fellow-ship of Reconciliation National Council to encourage it to form a task force to deal with the Nicaraguan war. I visited other peace groups and also teamed up with Cora Weiss of the Riverside Church Disarmament Program, who had been in our delegation to Nicara-gua. She was the moving force behind the establishment of an office in Washington to organize groups of Americans to visit Nicaragua. It has been my belief that the constant visiting by such fact-finding groups is the only thing that kept the Reagan administration from all-out war against Nicaragua.

In 1982 I also visited Maryknoll headquarters in New York to do some radio broadcasts about the war and discuss strategy.

When Ronald Reagan ordered the invasion of Grenada, we held a protest meeting of more than a hundred persons on November 6, 1983, in a black church in Kansas City, where, along with a Grenadian visitor, I spoke about the background of the Reagan action.

A group of us including Tom Fox, editor of the *National Catholic Reporter,* Ed Haase, Beth Seberger and at least sixty others, met January 7, 1984, at All Souls Unitarian Church to form an ad hoc committee in opposition to the C.I.A. war in Nicaragua. It was a committee largely drawn from peace and church groups and black organizations in Kansas City. I was elected chairperson and a year or so later asked Sister Kathleen Kenny to serve as co-chair.

In June 1984 I was made Professor Emeritus of Christian Ethics at Saint Paul School of Theology, and I continued teaching a course or two at the School and also taught several courses at the Baker University graduate program. From this point on I was less active in Kansas City and more active nationally, with much of my activity centered in the A.C.L.U. National Board, of which I had been a member from 1970 to 1997, and in Americans for Religious Liberty, of which I was elected president in 1987.

Chapter 8
The Case of Lieutenant Font

During the war in Vietnam I had an unusual opportunity to assist Lt. Louis Font in getting an honorable discharge from the Army. Font was a West Point honors graduate, the first and only West Point graduate up to that point to seek discharge as a selective objector. A selective objector refuses to participate in a specific war instead of all wars. Lt. Font had gone to the John F. Kennedy School of Government at Harvard as part of the Army's distinguished graduates program, where he had taken courses with Henry Kissinger, later the President's assistant for national security affairs. At West Point he graduated 31st in a class of 700 cadets, ranked first in foreign languages, second in law, and among the top ten in psychology, history and the social sciences.

Font wavered over a period of two years about the news of the Vietnam war, America's role in the destruction of that small country, the My Lai massacre, and finally turned to religion. "When I apply the Just War theories as laid down by St. Thomas Aquinas, St. Augustine and others, to me at a minimum the Vietnam war is rendered unjust by the vast scale and proportion of destruction deployed especially in a war characterized by the inability to distinguish combatants from non-combatants," Font said in his discharge application.

"The way my conscience forces me to see it -- the way I feel it -- the U.S. government is destroying another culture and in the process is destroying itself and its integrity," he continued. "For me to participate in any way in an immoral war is the most extreme form of violence to my conscience."

Font filed this discharge application on February 27, 1970, with the assistance of three American Civil Liberties Union lawyers. One of them, Marvin Karpatkin, with whom I served on the national board of ACLU, gave Font my name. The reason was a serious disagreement between Font and his parents in Kansas City, Kansas, over his action. He had phoned his parents on March 13 from

76

Cambridge, Massachusetts, to tell them he had gotten orders from the Pentagon to disenroll from Harvard University and report to Fort Meade, Maryland. That same night he called me in Kansas City, Missouri, to ask me to visit his parents and to try to explain his action and seek their support. They had worked to get him into West Point and desperately wanted him to have an Army career. I agreed to see them on Sunday the 15th.

In the meantime our family had a surprise visit from Rev. and Mrs. Lester Auman. Lester was a retired pastor of national prominence in the Methodist Church. He was a gentle person, then 79 years of age, who, despite his mild manner and pacifist convictions, had fought hard for progressive measures within the church. On Sunday, as I was about to leave to visit the Fonts as scheduled, my wife said, "Take Lester along." He was delighted to go, and promised to let me do the talking! The Font family received us and listened to my explanation, but were unconvinced. After almost an hour of discussion, Mr. Font said to Lester Auman: "Your face is familiar. Did you ever live on Long Island?" When Lester listed the several towns where he had served churches there, Mr. Font suddenly said: "We attended that church." Mrs. Font went for her family record book, and Louis Font's baptismal certificate had been signed by -- Rev. Lester Auman.

This seemed to them not only a very remarkable coincidence, but a miracle. Mrs. Font, a Puerto Rican woman, cried, and then laughed. From that point on they listened with understanding and were persuaded to support their son.

That was only the beginning, as Font, then at Fort Meade, was to be tried by a military court. I phoned Washington to talk to Herman Will, the executive of the Methodist Peace Division of the Board of Christian Social Concerns, and an old friend. His office was in the same building as that of the Methodist Commission on Chaplains. Herman talked to the head of that Commission, who phoned the Methodist chaplain at Fort Meade. He did not tell him what to do, but said that if he thought Font was sincere, the Methodist Church would back the chaplains' recommendation, if necessary, against the Army authorities. Font was interviewed by the Army psychiatrist, who pronounced him sane, and by the chaplain, Maj. Bill Whiteside, for an hour and a half. Afterward

Whiteside said Font was definitely sincere and his claim was based on religious belief. Font wrote me a report on March 24:

> Next is the officers' hearing called the 0-3 hearing. . . It is almost definite that we will ask you to appear; it would mean so much. I mentioned your name to Chaplain Whiteside and pointed out your supporting letter in the application, and he told me he had heard of you and had shaken your hand once or twice at different conferences but that you would probably not remember him. He read your letter and I am sure was quite impressed.

On April 14 I appeared at Fort Meade for the 0-3 hearing and was examined extensively before the hearing officer, Major Donald E. Cukjati, a Roman Catholic, about the medieval Just War theory and its modern application to conscientious objection in general, and the position of the United Methodist Church, the history of conscientious objection in America, as well as about Lt. Font. Major Cukjati said in his official report that Font was "sincere in his beliefs," but recommended that the discharge application be "disapproved" since selective objection is "not authorized under the provisions [of Army regulations]." When Font wrote me April 20 about the hearing, before Major Cukjati made his recommendation, he said:

> I spoke with Major Cukjati the morning after the hearing. Among other things he told me he had been most impressed by your testimony. I hope that makes your effort all the more worthwhile -- you traveled the longest distance, you were on the stand the longest, you spoke with me time and time again.

Unfortunately, the Major's recommendation prevailed against the weight of the testimony of five witnesses, including Dr. Paul Deats of Boston University and three professors from Harvard University, one of them also a U.S. Army major.

When the Department of the Army's Conscientious Objector Review Board took the case, Marvin Karpatkin, the A.C.L.U. General Counsel, said he was ready to take the case to Federal District Court in Baltimore if the application was denied. However, the Army took its time and on June 16, 1970, ruled that Font did not qualify as a conscientious objector because he "lacks the depth of sincerity" required and because "the applicant's claim is based on objection to a particular war" rather than to war itself. Font was ordered to attend training exercises at Fort Benning, Georgia, and from there to be sent to Vietnam.

His attorneys, Marvin Karpatkin and Michael Pollet, asked for a restraining order in the Federal District Court in Baltimore, and Font's orders were frozen until July 24, when a hearing on appeal was expected.

In the meantime there were a number of other developments. I wrote Marvin Karpatkin on June 15 that the church which the Font family attended was a part of the Kansas East Conference of the United Methodist Church.

Last week I had my membership transferred to that Conference (from the New York Conference), although not for this reason. Then I arranged to have the enclosed resolution on selective objection introduced. It was assigned to a committee to which I was also assigned. A former student of mine was in charge of making both assignments. After two days of committee discussion it was sent to the floor of the Conference, where it was adopted without obvious dissent on Friday, June 12. This means that you are now in a position to say that Louis Font has support for his position from the official church body of which his local church is a part.

On January 12, 1971, Font and four other officers formally requested a Court of Inquiry be convened to investigate alleged U.S. war crimes in Vietnam, and submitted to the Secretaries of the Army and Navy more than three hundred pages of testimony from Vietnam veterans claiming to have witnessed U.S. atrocities." This was reported in papers nationwide (*Kansas City Star,* January 13, 1971).

Font also preferred charges against Colonel A.W. Alexander, Post Commander at Fort Meade, for dereliction of duty with regard to the barracks conditions, with 85 supporting statements from enlisted men. He also preferred charges against Major General Robert G. Cuculello for assault and battery under Article 128 of the Uniform Code of Military Justice. The Army retaliated by making five charges against Lt. Font. Among them was a charge for entering a barracks belonging to another Command, and a charge for entering the headquarters building without the approval of the commanding officer. Each of the charges carried a five-year penalty.

In March 1971 I organized a committee in Greater Kansas City to secure the release of Font from the Army, and to seek dismissal of charges against him. The committee was a distinguished group including Girard Bryant, President of the Metropolitan Community College and former member of the Police Board, Rev. J.L. Garnett, director of the social action office of the Catholic Diocese of Kansas City, Missouri, Rev. John Stitz of the Archdiocese office in Kansas City, Kansas, Rev. Frederick Ackman of Old Mission Methodist Church, Rabbi Paul Levenson of Temple Beth El, and numerous other religious and secular leaders. This received publicity in the *Kansas City Star,* and letters began flowing in to various members of Congress. The headline in the *Star* said: "Committee Rallies to Font in Dispute with Army."

As a result of the interest in Font reflected by speeches by some members of Congress, the suit filed in Federal Court and Font's own trouble-making suits, the Army finally gave him an honorable discharge later in 1971. Of course, some additionally important factors in Font's case were the increasing and by then overwhelming public opinion against the war in Vietnam, the legal assistance of ACLU attorneys, and the support of the United Methodist Church. The Methodist Peace Division was headed then by Herman Will, who gave active support to persons of conscience.

After Font's discharge he studied law, married a lawyer, and is in private practice in Boston.

On January 22, 1978, Font wrote Lester Auman to thank him for a Christmas card and note to his parents. He summarized what had happened to him and concluded with these words:

I have a number of cases which I take for free. I try to treat all my clients in the same way that I was treated by the excellent ACLU-cooperating attorneys, and others who represented me. There is not a day goes by that I do not remember them, and their excellent representation. I also try to put forward the same ideas toward social progress that I learned from John Swomley, and from your example.

Font, of course, was not the only officer to file for conscientious objector status. There were others, including another United Methodist, Captain Robert Firehock, whose home was in Florida, and who wrote me at the recommendation of Louis Font on June 8, 1970. He had been a classmate of Font's at West Point, with an even higher rank in his graduating class, and was in a Master's degree program at Stanford University when he wrote me. He wrote: "I was raised a Methodist in a religiously active family. My father was a West Point graduate and a career officer, now retired for five years." Firehock asked me if he could come to Kansas City the weekend of June 20 for a visit and discussion. I wrote inviting him.

He wrote after the visit:

Thank you very much for your generous hospitality and patience last weekend. I thoroughly enjoyed meeting and visiting with you and your family. I know that I profited from our discussions, especially along the lines of preparing for consequences -- knowing you can accept the worst fate is a great source of strength.

Bob Firehock filed his claim for conscientious objector status on November 30, after having done further thought and reading, including Garth MacGregor's *New Testament Basis of Pacifism*. Marvin Karpatkin and his colleague, Michael Pollet, also represented him. I did not need to participate further in his securing conscientious objector status.

It was necessary to be involved in the tremendous movement against the war in Vietnam to understand the feeling about the atrocities committed there by U.S. military personnel and the turmoil this created for conscientious young men in the armed forces. Four officers, all West Point men, three of whom served in Vietnam, wrote a letter in the May 24, 1970, *Washington Post* supporting Font. They said:

We have earned between us one Silver Star and four Bronze Stars. We have seen the ideals of the Republic which we have sworn to defend perverted beyond recognition in the systematic destruction of another people's country. . . . In the name of the America of our hopes we join Lt. Font in saying -- No."

It is also necessary to remember how public opinion gradually turned against that war to realize why the Army could not simply ride roughshod over these men once they had made their decision and gone public with it in a church accustomed to supporting conscience, and with the American Civil Liberties Union giving them legal assistance.

Chapter 9
Europe, 1966

My first sabbatical from teaching at St. Paul was in Europe in 1966. It was a series of adventures which included a meeting with the East German Secretary of Church-State Affairs, dialogue with Communists in Prague, a dramatic session with a representative of the National Liberation Front of Vietnam in their European head-quarters in Prague, and an address to the Foreign Affairs Committee of the British House of Commons.

When our family left Kansas City at the end of February, 1966, public opposition to the war in Vietnam had barely begun. I had written an article in 1964 against the war, and had initiated action against it including a committee to oppose the war, vigils, and demonstrations in Kansas City. We had not been involved in any large demonstration until early March when we participated, just before sailing, in the first major demonstration in Washington. A night or two before that demonstration I spoke at a public meeting at Catholic University where Philip Berrigan participated in the panel discussion. He and his brother Daniel had not yet begun their public protests against war. In fact, Philip said that evening that he had been reading my regular newsletter, *Current Issues,* and was awakened to the need to speak publicly on the war and the military.

So the war in Vietnam was very much on my mind as we headed for Europe, although my principal purpose in going overseas was to encourage and assist in the formation of an Institute on Nonviolence in London at the request of the International Fellowship of Reconciliation. We sailed on the S.S. United States, arrived in LeHavre, and soon thereafter drove through Belgium, France, Spain and Switzerland before heading for London.

Probably my most important public meeting was in Brussels April 15-17, where I had been invited to address an international peace conference sponsored by the International F.O.R. I spoke about the war in Vietnam, and received invitations to Oslo, East and West Berlin, Prague, and Dortmund, Germany. In the audience was

Heinz Kloppenberg, who, next to Martin Niemoller, was the most influential leader of the German churches against World War II and the Hitler government. He introduced himself to me and asked if I would be interested in going to East Berlin at his expense to meet with the official in the Communist government of East Germany who was in charge of relations with the churches. He said this man believed the West German churches were a tool of the American churches, who were in turn instruments of the U.S. government, and hence agents of western imperialism. Heinz Kloppenberg wanted me to persuade this official that his picture of the churches was incorrect. I agreed to meet him in East Berlin.

Two months later after the appointment had been arranged, I took the train to Berlin. I did not realize until later that the East German official, Hans Siegewasser, and Kloppenberg had been interned in the same concentration camp during the war and had developed a mutual respect and admiration for each other in spite of their differing positions. Seigewasser had become Secretary of State for Church Affairs after the East German government was organized following the war.

Heinz and I entered a large room at the appointed hour on June 17 to find three men. One was Seigewasser; one of the others was a scribe who took down everything that was said. The third was a representative of the secret police, who evidently had some authority to check on the decisions of the Secretary for Church Affairs. After the introductions I began the conversation by asking Siegewasser about the status of the churches in East Germany, whether they had become more conservative or more progressive under his leadership. He indicated that the churches were showing more interest in peace and social justice on the one hand, and on the other were showing more understanding of the position of the state. He used as an illustration the Berlin Wall. He said the reaction to the wall was not negative but a recognition that the state needed to respond to West Germany. He justified the wall on the ground that it could have been avoided if West Berlin authorities had not flown out of Berlin those without valid passports.

I asked a question about propaganda for atheism and was told that there was no organization in East Germany to promote atheism. After I questioned him in a friendly way for about a half hour, I paused to ask if he had any questions to ask me about churches in the U.S. He had seemed remarkably well informed about churches in Europe, but raised many questions about the churches in the U.S., including the attitude toward the war in Vietnam and toward rights for Negroes. I told him that about 50,000 church leaders, both clergy and lay, had served some time in Southern jails during the civil rights campaign, and also that no prominent clergypersons except Cardinal Spellman and Billy Graham were publicly and verbally supporting the war in Vietnam. This discussion made a real impression on the Secretary and I had a chance to describe the American concept of separation of church and state, and how important it was for the churches to avoid financial subsidy by the government in order to remain independent of it.

During the conversation I became aware how important the social witness of the churches in the West is to the well-being of churches in the East. Afterwards I reflected on what seemed to me to be increasingly evident, that it is more important for churches in the West to present a different view of the church than to criticize their counterparts in Eastern Europe. We do not understand in detail the circumstances under which churches have had to live in the East, and under those circumstances criticism is not helpful, whereas example may persuade.

Heinz Kloppenberg, however, took advantage of a lull in our conversation to raise three questions with the Secretary, which he had not shared with me in advance but which were apparently his real reason for inviting me to East Berlin. He asked first for permission to send into East Germany from West Germany 3,000 copies of a biography or autobiography of the Lutheran Archbishop Dibelius. There was a long discussion between Siegewasser and the representative of the secret police. Finally the Secretary said, "Granted." The next question was to ask permission for 3,000 copies of *Die Junge Kirche,* a young adult German church magazine, to be sent regularly into East Germany. After another discussion with the secret police agent, this too was granted. I have forgotten Kloppenberg's third request, but it was also granted.

We were both pleased as we walked away from the building where our discussion had taken place. I had actually engaged in a successful negotiation with a Communist official, had helped in accomplishing an important mission, and had learned a great deal in the process. Kloppenberg, who was also the West German secretary of the Fellowship of Reconciliation, was a remarkable person, trusted and respected by people in both Eastern and Western Europe.

Kloppenberg went shortly thereafter to see Helmut Gollwitzer, the well-known theologian, who taught in the Berlin Free University, to urge him to find some promising German student who wanted to study in the United States and who would teach me German. I had not suggested this to him. He evidently hoped that on my next visit to Europe I would be able to lecture in or at least converse in German.

Gollwitzer wrote me and arranged for a talented and most congenial young woman, Helga Krüger, to come and live with our family in Kansas City. She became truly a member of our family and a favorite of our three small children. She attended school and graduated with honors at the Saint Paul School of Theology, for which we provided a scholarship and her transportation. She went on for graduate study at Union Theological Seminary in New York, where she earned a doctorate and met and married a former Catholic priest, Tom Day. Helga Krüger Day and her husband now live in Berlin where she has served as a pastor and he as university Protestant chaplain. I visited them and their two small children in the fall of 1985. However, during the time Helga lived with us I was unfortunately too busy traveling, speaking, writing and teaching to spend the time studying German, and hence never learned to speak it.

During 1966 my work in London was largely speaking, writing, and consulting with peace leaders, although on several occasions I crossed the Channel for meetings in Europe. While in London in early May I received my first trans-Atlantic phone call. It was from my successor as F.O.R. executive secretary, Alfred Hassler, who asked me to drop everything and go to Prague immediately. He wanted me to meet with the National Liberation Front of Vietnam representatives in their main European headquarters to see if I could arrange for the first delegation of American church leaders to visit North Vietnam. He also wanted me to convince the N.L.F. that the anti-war movement in the U.S. was still too weak to be able to end the war. It was already afternoon, and the Czech Embassy had closed for the day. Nevertheless I went to the Embassy and beat on the door until a custodian finally appeared. I convinced him with much effort to bring me some official and, after talking to several persons, was admitted to the Embassy and given a visa for the next day.

I had already reserved a seat on the first morning plane to Prague, and went immediately on my arrival to the N.L.F. headquarters, which was on an upper floor of an old building not far from the main shopping center of the city. It was one of seven missions outside of Vietnam. The others were located in Algiers, Cairo, Havana, Jakarta, Moscow, Peking, and East Berlin. While all of the missions were said to be of equal status, the head of the mission in Prague, Prof. Nguyen Van Hieu, was the former Secretary-General of the N.L.F., and therefore very influential. Unfortunately he was not in Prague, having gone to Berlin for a visit to the N.L.F. office there.

During five hours of conversation in English with Pham Van Chuong, who was in charge in the absence of the head of the mission, I learned a great deal about the N.L.F., including its organizational structure and its policy for the future. I did not succeed in my main objective, getting permission for a delegation to visit North Vietnam. On several occasions I stressed the fact that the U.S. peace movement was not strong enough to end the war. Each time I was told that their intelligence in the U.S. was very good and that they knew what I was saying was accurate. Then, to emphasize the point, Chuong excused himself, went to the next room where I heard him open and close a file drawer. He came back into the room where I was waiting and laid on the table in front of me the latest copy of *Ramparts* magazine, which, I believed, had not yet reached newsstands in America. I asked him how he had gotten it; all he said was, "from Hawaii."

I discussed two possibilities for ending the war, and was told simply that both of those questions would be referred to the Central Committee. Then I proposed nonviolent resistance. We discussed the illustrations of the use of nonviolence by Buddhists against the South Vietnamese government of President Ky, but to no avail. My notes at the time said: "There seemed to be not only a misunderstanding of what nonviolent resistance entailed but too great reliance on guerrilla warfare and too great faith in ultimate victory to pursue the discussion."

The conversation ended on an appeal to me, to the Fellowship of Reconciliation and other religious peace groups to raise our voices against the use of chemical and gas warfare. "Gas," he said, "has been standard equipment for U.S. troops, and soldiers can use gas grenades without specific authorization." He referred to deaths resulting from supposedly non-lethal gases and quoted a January 12, 1966, Reuters dispatch from Saigon that said "non-toxic gas and smoke being used against the guerrillas in underground tunnels had killed one Australian soldier and sent six others to hospitals." He added that they were wearing gas masks at the time. I walked away from the conference meditating about truth and propaganda and the courtesy with which I was treated.

I went immediately to the Comenius Theological School to talk to two old friends, Jan Lochman and Joseph Smolek, whom I had entertained in Kansas City and had known on other occasions. I spent the night as their guest. They also told me about the Christian-Communist dialogues that had been taking place in Prague between members of their faculty and leading Communist intellectuals. At the meeting preceding my arrival the dean of the Comenius Faculty, Joseph Hromadka, had lectured on prayer at the request of the Communists. He had spoken for two and a half hours. At my suggestion, he arranged for me to have a conference with one of their dialogue group, Julius Tomin, who was later to be active in the 1969 abortive effort to change the situation in Czechoslovakia by democratization and freedom from Soviet rule.

Tomin told me that the dialogue was not a tactic in a struggle between Christian and Communist. He said, "The fact that we have lived side by side with no mutual interest to break the barrier between us is itself a reason to break the barrier. We now talk about anything with an incredible freedom." Tomin indicated that the Marxist intellectuals had set for themselves three requisites for the dialogue. The first was freedom from preconceptions based on Marx's ideas of 19th Century Christianity -- in other words, openness for the unexpected. When I asked how it was possible for those who claim to have the "true religion" to be genuinely open to others, the answer was: "Marxism does not claim to have the truth, but the best way of coming to or seeking the truth."

The second requisite was that dialogue forbids the use of violence or power against the dialogue partner if only because power destroys the possibility of honest discussion. I noted at the time that "recognition that there are areas of life incompatible with violence or power represents a deepening of Marxist insight."

In the third place he said dialogue must involve an effort to see the optimal possibilities for oneself, the other person, society, and the world. "The Marxists ought to oppose Christianity only if they have a full guarantee that they can give concrete Christians as persons a more optimal inner life and deeper living than they are able to attain as Christians." Atheism without giving people a higher purpose "only contributes to the sickness of society. This hurts the health and development of a socialist country."

Jan Lochman of the Comenius Faculty added another perspective: "If there is no contact with people who think a different way, you lose your own freshness."

While in Prague I also paid a visit to the office of the Christian Peace Conference and met J.J. Ondra, their executive, who had been a conscientious objector during World War II.

Upon my return to London I prepared a major lecture on "Justice, Revolution, and Violence" to give in Holland. That lecture was reprinted several times in periodicals, one of which was the British *Reconciliation Quarterly.* On another trip to Holland a few days later, I met a Dominican priest, Andre Dekker, who was on the theological faculty in Zwolle. I spent the night in his parents' home in Arnhem and the next day at the Dominican Klooster in Zwolle. I met with the faculty for a discussion and later spent five hours with my counterpart, Professor Arntz, who taught Moral Theology (the Catholic term for Christian Ethics). Professor Arntz and I spent our time in intensive discussion of the Just War, non-violence, and other topics, since he was engaged in major writing about the Just War.

I discussed with Andre Dekker the possibility of his coming to the United States. After we returned he did come and was interviewed for a faculty position at Saint Paul School of Theology. We offered him a teaching position but he subsequently decided to accept an offer at a college in Illinois.

In London, British Friends invited me to a luncheon on May 16 at William Penn house to speak on Vietnam to a group of organizational leaders, professors in Asian studies, and one professor of military science. Following that meeting, Kenneth Lee of the Friends Peace Committee phoned Philip Noel-Baker to suggest that we discuss Vietnam. Noel-Baker was chair of the Foreign Affairs

Committee of the House of Commons, which was controlled by the Labour Party. He was also a Nobel Peace Prize winner, largely for his work in the field of disarmament. It was he who persuaded Kruschev to make his 1959 United Nations disarmament address.

Philip Noel-Baker's secretary phoned to invite me to be his dinner guest on May 19 at the House of Commons Dining Room. We met and talked from 7:30 to 10:30 p.m., when he was called to a division in the House. During our conversation he told me he had read my book, *The Military Establishment,* published in 1964, and had been receiving and reading for years the *Current Issues* and *Disarmament News* that I had been writing. He regretted that I spent more time on analyses of current issues than on disarmament issues, which he judged more important. We discussed Vietnam chiefly in the context of what could be done to end the war. Before I left he invited me to speak to the Foreign Affairs Committee at its next meeting on May 24.

On May 24, with about fifteen Members of Parliament present, I spoke for twenty minutes on the topic "What Britain can do to help end the war in Vietnam" and answered questions for at least another twenty minutes. In brief I outlined my understanding of military influence over U.S. foreign policy, the military strategy regarding Vietnam, the various U.S. rebuffs to peace negotiation efforts, the President's rejection of mutual de-escalation during the bombing pause when Vietnamese troops were pulled back, and ended with a brief report on the recent action of the Danish Government to try to end the war. I told them of my discussion with the National Liberation Front representative in Prague.

A former Secretary of War was on the Committee. He said: "Aren't you aware that more than half of all modern industry in the British Isles is owned by Americans?" Another M.P. said, "Aren't you aware that the British pound is bolstered by the American dollar?" This was their way of saying that the British government could not take an independent initiative on foreign policy.

There were numerous other questions about my proposal that Britain withdraw its support from the U.S. war effort, about the anti-war demonstrations in the U.S., what would prevent a Communist takeover in Southeast Asia if the U.S. withdraws. We were unable to continue beyond the allotted time because I had to leave in order to catch a train to Oxford where I was speaking that night. I saw

Philip Noel-Baker twice after that, once in the U.S. at the United Nations, and once in Tokyo in 1981 at a World Peace Conference sponsored by Japanese Buddhists. Noel-Baker was well past ninety years of age in 1981, but remembered our meeting at the House of Commons. He gave a magnificent address without notes at the Tokyo conference. He was one of the few statesmen in the twentieth century truly dedicated to achieving disarmament and an end to the war system.

We returned to the United States in July with a new Volvo that we had purchased for $2,100. It was our first new car, and I drove it for fourteen years.

An overseas experience was to become my typical sabbatical from teaching at Saint Paul. I learned more by action, dialogue, interviews, and involvement than by formal study at some institution. My study and research seemed to be a preparation for speaking or writing or for difficult encounters in which my first-hand experience would be useful.

Chapter 10
Argentina and Brazil, 1969

A valued friend of many years, Richard Chartier, had been teaching in the Facultad Evangelica de Teología in Buenos Aires for about ten years. He had written urging me to take a sabbatical or part of one to come there and teach. It was an exciting offer which we couldn't refuse. Although I had been to various countries in Central America, including Costa Rica, I had not learned to speak Spanish. I took an intensive crash course with Berlitz in Chicago and headed South on July 1, 1969, with the family, stopping for a few days in each country on the West Coast en route to Argentina.

In Mexico by chance I met a young revolutionary, Virgilio Vasquez, who had been in a violent student demonstration where seventeen of his friends had been killed. He became our guide, and helped carry our baby girl as we went sightseeing. Years later he came to Kansas City to study at Saint Paul School of Theology, in spite of his bitterness about "Yankee imperialism." There he took several of my courses, including one on Christian pacifism. He became a pacifist, and is now a pastor in Laredo, Texas, and a friend with whom I always hope to keep in touch.

From Mexico we went to Guatemala, where we had our first sight of government guards carrying sub-machine guns, to Costa Rica, and to Panama, where I had some meetings, and then on to Colombia, Ecuador and Peru. In Lima, although I was scheduled to preach in the American Church, I did not do so because Braniff overflew Quito and made us wait for the next day's plane. Nonetheless, two Catholic priests who had traveled the distance from Chimbote were waiting for us, eager to discuss nonviolence and what they might do in a situation where local Communist labor leaders had already threatened their lives.

After seeing the magnificent Inca ruins at Macchu Picchu we went by train over a 15,600 foot mountain pass to the Indian city of Huancayo, where we experienced a destructive earthquake which toppled buildings and destroyed the city's water supply.

After several other stops in Peru we crossed Lake Titicaca by steamer and eventually arrived in La Paz, Bolivia, one of the highest cities in the world, with Indians the most visible part of the city's population. In La Paz I met and had an interesting discussion of American imperialism and the military-industrial complex in America with Bishop Mortimer Arias. He decided on the spur of the moment to arrange a meeting for the next day, where I spoke to Methodist clergy and lay workers on issues of empire and war. Later he became a theology professor in the United States, having been forced out of Bolivia by the government because of his strong support of Bolivian tin miners. We remain friends to this day.

From La Paz we flew to Santiago, Chile, for a round of interviews before going to Buenos Aires, where I would be teaching in the leading Protestant theological school in Latin America, with students from all over the continent. Our children went to a school in Buenos Aires where classes were taught in Spanish in the morning and English in the afternoon. The course I taught in the School of Theology with sixteen students enrolled was entitled "U.S. Power and Policy in the Twentieth Century." One important section dealt with Latin American policy, and included "Solutions for Latin America." Another dealt with ideologies and strategies for social change. In addition to teaching, I lectured on several occasions to the faculty and student body and spoke in various other places in Argentina and Uruguay.

Soon after our arrival I became involved in a little non-violent group of Argentinians who met once a month at the theological seminary, with my friend Chartier also involved. One of their leaders, Isabel de Sousa, had been arrested July 2, along with many others, under the State of Siege proclamation which was for all practical purposes a form of martial law. During the State of Siege, all constitutional procedures such as *habeas corpus* were invalid. Although there was no provision in the Constitution for the State of Siege, the military president, General Juan Carlos Onganía, imposed it on July 1, prior to our arrival in Argentina.

Mrs. Sousa was an active Catholic lay leader, president for twenty years of the Catholic Action group in her parish. She had gone to a conference in Montreal, Canada, where the war in Vietnam was discussed. This aroused the suspicions of the police. She lived in a small apartment behind the little store where she worked. The police raided her apartment and discovered sleeping bags and tents belonging to her nephews who used them for camping. They also found lists of those involved in the nonviolent action group as well as those active in Argentine solidarity with Vietnam, some of whom were alleged to be Communists. The police made no official charge against her at her arrest, but told her informally it was because of her identification as a lay person with the "priests of the Third World," who advocated revolutionary change in Latin America's social structure.

When I met with the nonviolent action group they wanted to gain Mrs. Sousa's release from prison, but some were afraid even to write a letter to the government on her behalf because they were not economically prepared to spend months or years in prison without provision for their families. Even the lawyers who intervened on behalf of arrested persons were themselves arrested and five were known to be still in jail at the time of our meeting.

After a long discussion I proposed a procedure for getting her out of jail. It included a 24-hour vigil at her parish church with an open letter to the Roman Catholic Archbishop Aramburu, who had once given her a diploma for her study of the social doctrines of the Catholic Church. About a hundred and fifty persons, including the Swomleys, attended the vigil and signed the open letter to the Archbishop. We said in the letter everything we wanted to say to the President, General Onganía, about her innocence and our request for her return. We had arranged with a major tabloid daily to feature the letter and vigil in its centerpiece. Within about a month after our action Mrs. Sousa was released.

The churches were the only places in Argentina where one could speak openly and politically in criticism of the government or the social system. On one occasion when I was invited to preach in the large Central Methodist Church on September 14, I preached a strong sermon critical of social conditions in both the U.S. and in Argentina. An American missionary couple serving in Brazil, who were at the service that morning, told me: "If you preach like that in Brazil you will never preach again. They will pick you up." Brazil had an even more repressive government than Argentina.

Everywhere I went to speak, there were "priests of the Third World" who later called themselves Christians of the Third World in order to involve Protestants. They did want to revolutionize Latin

America, but had their doubts about violence. They eagerly asked me about non-violence. However, when I lectured on November 14 in the large Roman Catholic theological school in Córdoba in the north of the country, the most Catholic city in Argentina, their heroes were Castro and Che Guevara. I criticized Castro for not installing democracy in Cuba and for not having free elections. One student among the more than five hundred in the room, stood to interrupt me. He said: "In Cuba there are meetings at the block level in cities and at the village level where the people discuss their needs and desires. Those decisions are passed up to larger community meetings and from there to urban and larger levels. Then they are turned over to Castro, who simply proclaims them as the will of the people."

I responded by saying I could understand how they as Catholics might believe this, because the laity in local churches discussed their needs, the priests passed these on to the bishops, who passed them on to the Cardinals, who passed them on to the Pope, and the Pope simply proclaimed the will of the people. I knew of course that it didn't happen that way, and so did the students. All over the room there were cries: "The Pope is a dictator!" I became convinced that in that atmosphere it was possible to criticize the Pope and probably Jesus, but not Castro or Guevara. On the other hand, when I talked about Gandhi and Martin Luther King, they showed the same kind of admiration for their nonviolent leadership as they did for Castro or Che Guevara.

In fact, students all over Latin America idolized Guevara, and his picture was plastered over every available surface in public parks and university walls.

There were numerous incidents in Buenos Aires. One day a news photographer snapped my picture outside the U.S. Embassy giving a letter to President Nixon to an official there on the day of the large "Moratorium" protest in the U.S. against the war in Vietnam. It appeared the next day, October 16, in the *Buenos Aires Herald,* the English-language paper.

On another occasion at a little vegetable market where I had been a steady shopper for two months, the owner suddenly shouted at me, blaming me for the war in Vietnam. I explained my position to him and he was friendly thereafter.

In another instance a pastor whom I met said he would like to arrange a meeting for me, but he did not want to be known as a "Gringo" follower. There was a great deal of hostility to the United States because of its imperialist policies and the war in Vietnam, though generally this was not directed at U.S. visitors. However, a group of chain stores owned by Rockefeller interests was burned when Nelson Rockefeller came to Buenos Aires while we were there.

I was invited to speak in Montevideo, Uruguay, at a public meeting, and also at a Mennonite theological seminary in the same city in early September. My translator at the public meeting was Emilio Castro, who later became the Secretary of the World Council of Churches. After the meeting I met with Uruguayan "priests of the Third World" (so-called because they wanted no part of either the capitalist or Communist world) who eagerly plied me with questions about nonviolent resistance. Those priests were a very small group in Uruguay. Even in Argentina they numbered only about 400 out of about 4,000 priests in the whole country.

In spite of a great deal of interest in social change, there were no significant revolutionary movements in Argentina or most of South America. The two groups with the most potential for revolution were the Communist Party and the Peronistas, but neither group seemed interested in revolution. The Peronist-controlled unions did call several general strikes while we were in Buenos Aires, in spite of the repressive State of Siege.

Other than these strikes and some other union opposition to government, the most militant activity while we were in Buenos Aires was an anti-war protest which I helped to organize. I had gathered signatures from U.S. citizens in Argentina to a petition to be presented to the American Embassy against the war in Vietnam. We planned a march or demonstration on a pedestrian street, Avenida Florida, on which the Embassy was situated. Since no more than two or three people were permitted, under the State of Siege, to gather anywhere on the streets, we thought a two-block walk of a hundred or more people was all we could manage. We prepared leaflets and openly announced our plans. We also indicated that those who did not want to participate could meet in the Methodist Church not far from the Embassy, where we would gather for a meeting after the march.

When six of us who had done the planning arrived at the appointed place on Florida, we discovered police vans and khaki-clad armed police had been stationed at the block where the march was to begin. I suggested we go to a nearby restaurant to alter our plans. At the restaurant I proposed a street meeting with our group of six asking the chief of police questions, loud enough for our march participants to hear. We went to the first police van and asked if we could talk to the chief. We were told he was at the other end of Florida several blocks away. We were given permission to go there to talk with him.

As we started down the street, we heard voices and feet behind us. About two hundred people had started to march, holding aloft pieces of paper they had taken from their pockets and unfolded as banners. The six of us moved into position ahead of them. We heard a shot from the rear and then saw a line of military police walking toward us, each armed with a cocked revolver in one hand and a "billy club" in the other. Officers behind them began lobbing tear gas canisters over their heads into our midst. I put my hands above my head so that my arms could protect my head from the clubs, something I learned from the civil rights campaign in the U.S. Argentina was unaccustomed to nonviolent demonstrations. The young policemen's hands were shaking because they feared being hurt by the crowd. When they saw my hands were empty, they made room for me to pass between two of the police. Richard Chartier on my right was clubbed, as were others. However, one man on each end did an end-run around the police. These two Argentine Communists each grabbed an elbow, picked me up, and ran with me out of the block.

When we got to the Methodist Church, there were already almost five hundred people waiting, with more coming. There were two speakers, one of them a Communist, and myself. Since the Soviet Union had recently invaded Czechoslovakia, I criticized Soviet violence there, as well as U.S. violence in Vietnam, much to the dismay of the Communist speaker, who was only prepared to indict the U.S. for its actions in Vietnam. After the speaking I went to the rear of the room to greet people, and met a woman who identified herself to me as working for the F.B.I. She was the secretary to John Wachter, the legal attache at the Embassy. We had a brief discussion, because she did not understand why I, a theological professor and a friend of William C. Sullivan, assistant director of the F.B.I., was doing these things.

The police were so intent on breaking up the march to the Embassy that they made few if any arrests at the time. News reporters, however, interviewed participants and published their names. During the next few weeks police began arresting those whose names were in the newspapers. My name was so garbled by Spanish-speaking reporters as to be unrecognizable. We left the country on schedule without my being imprisoned.

When I went to Latin America I carried with me a letter from Robert Hoyt, then the editor of *The National Catholic Reporter* (*NCR*), which asked for me "the usual courtesies and facilities made available to newspapers and magazine correspondents." From time to time I sent the *NCR* stories or interviews. Recently I came across one of those stories in the September 3, 1969, *NCR* which carried no byline as the writer (myself) had asked for "anonymity because he has been advised that he could be expelled from the country for this report."

During the week prior to our leaving in November, a Brazilian student living in Argentina, Sergio Schneider, asked to talk with me, and then arranged a meeting with the most distinguished scientist in Brazil, a courageous man who nevertheless did not want me to reveal his name because of the danger to those he left behind in Brazil. We talked for more than an hour about the torture of Brazilians by police and military personnel. Then he asked me if I would agree to be the person in the United States with whom he could communicate about torture after he returned. This would involve his sending me the news clippings and other information as well as emergency letters so I could organize public opinion to secure the release of political prisoners. I agreed to cooperate.

We worked out a code for correspondence and he told me he would never send me anything more than once from the same address. I was never to write to him or to his address but could reach him when necessary through his secretary at her home address. I did receive information from him and in a few cases was able to be helpful. The most unusual one was the case of Dr. Ernst Hamburger, a prominent Brazilian physicist, a Jew, a humanist, a professor and Acting President of the Brazilian Society of Physics.

Dr. Hamburger and his wife were apprehended away from home while their small children were home. His wife became hysterical about the children and after a few days was released. I received an air mail letter and the same day sent a letter to members of a world physicist organization and to American physicists, names I had located in a Kansas City library, telling the story of Dr. Hamburger and his wife, and asking letters and telegrams to go to the President of Brazil, Brazilian embassies, and the Secretary General of the Pan American Union asking his release. I understand that the response was tremendous and before long I received word of his release.

Sergio Schneider, who had initiated this process, came to the United States in 1970 and together with his wife stayed in our home for a time while trying with others to launch the *Brazilian Information Bulletin* which I agreed to co-sponsor. It was published for a number of years and Sergio joined its staff in Berkeley for a time. He took over the correspondence with the Brazilian scientist and eventually returned to Brazil. At that point letters were addressed to us via my wife's maiden name, Carpenter.

On our return to the U.S. we visited Brazil. We spent the last part of November in Sao Paulo and Rio de Janeiro. I met with labor leaders, with church social action persons, and others at meetings arranged by Para Iba, the Methodists' social action leader, who later occupied a leading position with the World Council of Churches. From these people I learned about the very harsh conditions in Brazil and with them I discussed possible ways of dealing with some of the problems. Probably my biggest learning experience came while we were staying at the Instituto Central do Poro in Rio as guests of Marion Way. That Institute was at the foot of a mountain on a very high hill, on the top of which about 60,000 poor people were living. The rich in Rio occupied the coastal or beach areas, whereas the poor had the view of the sea from the mountains. I wanted to visit that area but was told it was too dangerous for foreigners. Even the Catholic priest feared to stay overnight there.

I persuaded a former resident of the area to take me there early one morning. I saw shanty houses constructed with wood and tin. There was no sanitation. Urine and other sewage ran in streams through sections of that urban slum. There were six water faucets for the whole area, and there were long lines night and day of chiefly women and children waiting to fill old oil or gasoline cans with water to take back to their huts. They called the area ironically a "favela," which literally translated means "country club."

We left the capital of the country, Brasilia, on December 3, spent a few days in Trinidad, two in Caracas, and four in Puerto Rico, arriving in Kansas City just before Christmas. We were met and transported home by our friend Lewis Berg, who offered me a new-born toy-collie-mix puppy, which I picked up Christmas Eve to surprise the children on Christmas morning. We promptly named her "Chica," Spanish for "little girl."

Chapter 11
Uuder Martial Law in the Philippines

President Ferdinand Marcos proclaimed martial law in the Philippines on September 21, 1972. The announced reason for doing so was to end Communist subversion and widespread crime. These were serious problems. However, the real reason was rooted in the history of U.S.-Philippine relations. The U.S. Congress in 1946 had granted political independence to the Philippines, its former protectorate, and had passed a trade act which gave U.S. business firms the right to use, exploit and develop any and all natural resources, including land, and the operation of public utilities in the Philippines. The Philippine Supreme Court had decided in 1972 that U.S. citizens and business firms had no legal right to acquire land after 1946. The Court also ruled that all parity rights granted in 1946 to U.S. business would expire in 1974.

In addition, the Philippine Congress had planned the expropriation of all U.S. holdings by 1974. The U.S.-based multinational corporations were therefore the most immediate beneficiaries of martial law, because President Marcos nullified the Supreme Court decision, dissolved the nationalist Congress, and took away the various freedoms that the people could have used to protest his decisions. On September 27, 1972, the American Chamber of Commerce assured Marcos of business support for martial law. Marcos told *U.S. News & World Report,* issued October 26, 1972, that "we will offer as much incentive as is possible, and foreign capital will be protected. There will be no confiscation while I am President."

I was invited to teach social ethics, during a short sabbatical, at Union Theological Seminary in the Philippines after martial law had been proclaimed. Shortly after I had accepted the invitation, a copy of the decree entitled "Limitation on Academic Freedom of Teachers" was sent to me. Among the restrictions or prohibitions were the following: "Discourse or discussions on subject matter relating to

101

political or allied issues that tend to create or lead to disorder, chaos, or confusion in their students or audience."

Another of the seven academic prohibitions was "criticism against the authorities and the policies issued or programs instituted by them." I was not asked by Union Seminary to agree to abide by these, but was warned that a violation would be cause for my dismissal by the government.

I had decided to take our family with me to the Philippines, and had raised some money to make this possible. A manufacturer of contraceptives in St. Louis gave me a grant of $1,000 in return for doing some population studies in the Philippines. We left New York May 24, 1973, on a huge Air India plane. The Gandhi Peace Foundation had scheduled three meetings where I was to speak. One of the meetings wherein I discussed "Nonviolence and the U.S. Racial Scene" was chaired by India's leading educator, Dr. J.P. Naik, Secretary of the Indian Council of Social Science Research.

After a few days in Bangkok, a brief stop in Saigon, and two days in Hong Kong, we arrived in Tokyo and were met at the airport by a representative of the Japan Council of Churches and taken to the Methodist Guest House. I learned then for the first time that he had, without consulting me, arranged fifteen speaking engagements for me, among them a convocation address at the Japan International Christian University, an address to the faculty of Doshisha University in Kyoto, an assembly at the Palmore Institute in Kobe, and an evening public meeting in Hiroshima. At that meeting there were three survivors of the atom bombing of the city. The next day I preached to the group of Protestant and Catholic missionaries in that city and surrounding area. We were profoundly moved, as everyone is who visits Hiroshima, but even more so because of the survivors we met and the plastic surgeon who presided at my meeting and who had been involved in repairing so many survivors.

On June 30 we arrived in Manila and were met by the President of the Seminary, Emerito Nacpil, and three faculty members. We drove for over an hour to the Seminary campus about twenty-five miles south of Manila at Dasmarinas, Cavite province. The seminary was isolated, without a store, post office, bank or anything else.

My assignments were to teach a basic course on Christian Ethics, one dealing with Communism and Revolution, and to team-teach with two Filipino professors a course on The Church in Philippine Society. The librarian, Marian Kline, an American and former colleague in the Fellowship of Reconciliation in the 1940s, had removed all books dealing with Communism, revolution, and biographies of Marx, Lenin, and other Communists from the shelves when martial law was declared. Some libraries had been visited by military officers and everything "subversive" had been carted away. I persuaded her to put some of these books on a special reserve shelf with the rest in cartons in her office to which I had access.

In a letter written in August 12 to colleagues in Kansas City I wrote:

In my class on Christian Attitudes Toward Communism and Revolution there is a Maoist who keeps me on my toes with his party-line interpretations.

When I came I was warned that there might be a political agent in the classroom. In fact, one of the team teachers on several occasions in the Church and Philippine Society class had pleaded with the class for freedom of discussion and asked that no one inform on his brothers. I am now relatively convinced that there are no government agents in any of my classes. The one person I suspected as a possibility now seems quite open.

But we live constantly under an awareness that the government has virtually unlimited power. There is a controlled press. It is unsafe to criticize the government while riding in a taxi. People have been driven directly to the Philippine Constabulary and sent to a detention center.

Aside from teaching, I was asked to give four public lectures -- one on "Ideology," one on "Power," one on "Liberation," and one on "The New Morality, or Situation Ethics." I was also asked to lecture to the faculty, to give eight talks in chapel, and to participate in some informal sessions with students at the adjacent Philippine Christian College and at the seminary.

In July one of the Filipino instructors took me to visit Carmona, a resettlement town of 8,000 families. The Marcos government, shortly after martial law was declared, bulldozed some slum and squatter sections of Manila and moved the piles of wood and tin to

Carmona about twenty-five miles from Manila and about five miles from the seminary campus. The people had to reconstruct their huts and recover their existence. Only a few wells were dug or drilled, and jobs were virtually non-existent. Each family had a tiny plot of ground for a garden on which to eke out an existence. Families of six, eight, ten and twelve children lived in unshaded huts of about ten feet square. I saw some small children in crude hammocks hanging from a wall. Malnutrition and disease were all too apparent. But the poor were out of sight in Carmona, and, as my friend observed, "Marcos is further down the road toward the goal of a 'beautiful Manila'."

During my free time I began the practice of seeking interviews with prominent people in Manila. The most important was with Senator Jovito Salonga, the leading opponent of martial law who was not in a concentration camp. Senator Salonga, a prominent lawyer who later came to the United States in 1986 at the request of President Corazon Aquino to try to recover the billions of dollars that the Marcos family took to the United States, lived by a medical miracle. He was speaking at a public political rally before Marcos was elected President, when bombs were thrown and the place machine-gunned. He was rushed to the hospital where a score of surgeons worked to save his life. He and many others believed that Marcos was involved in the bombing. Salonga was not in detention under martial law, possibly for medical reasons, though I suspect his friend General Ramos may have protected him. Brigadier General Fidel Ramos was a West Point graduate who commanded the Philippine Constabulary, a branch of the Philippine armed forces.

In the course of my first meeting with Salonga in September, we discussed martial law, civil liberties, and the future of the Philippines. Finally he took a chance and said: "There are only three ways to end martial law. The first is the natural death of the President . . . " He paused, and I added, "The second is the unnatural death of Marcos." He smiled and said, "The third is bloody revolution." I said, "No Senator, there is a fourth way." He leaned forward and asked, "What is it?" I described my research for my book *Liberation Ethics,* which includes an analysis of violent and non-violent revolutions, and told him revolution was possible without violence. He said, "I must have that book."

He told me he had just finished reading a book by Reinhold Neibuhr and considered himself a believer in Niebuhr's "Christian Realism," which justified the use of armed violence as the lesser of two evils in which the other evil was submission to tyranny. However, he asked his pastor, Cirilo Rigos, a minister in a large Manila church of the United Church of Christ, to go to the seminary library for a copy, as I had none with me and was soon to leave for two weeks of lectures at Silliman University in Dumaguete on the island of Negros.

When I returned, I was invited immediately to lunch at Senator Salonga's home. When I entered his door he said to his five guests, "Gentlemen, this is our guest of honor." His five guests included his pastor, three other leading Protestant clergy in Manila, and José Calderón, an influential businessman. Salonga told me he had read *Liberation Ethics* and had read portions of it to each of the others. He proposed a discussion of its possible application to the Philippines. Toward the end of a three-hour discussion I proposed "a church-state confrontation with the Marcos government" and a regular meeting group of Catholic and Protestant clergy to study non-violent resistance and to develop strategies for the Manila scene. By the time I left the Philippines the group had grown to 150. They developed some interesting methods of resistance. Among them were Open Letters to President Marcos signed by prominent religious leaders, a mass boycott of compulsory election participation in Marcos' referendum of his continuation in office, and a mass meeting in and outside the Catholic Cathedral, when Cardinal Sin read a pastoral letter about the treatment of Catholic religious prisoners. In each of the above instances there was remarkable success. One of the Open Letters led to Marcos' pledge of free speech and debate during his proposed "public endorsement" of his remaining in office. The boycott, as I recall, led to more than a million abstentions; and thousands, including non-Catholics, filled the Cathedral and the square outside in protesting the treatment of political prisoners. There were other actions which I did not record.

However, since I was not in the Philippines at the time of the massive nonviolent demonstrations that forced Marcos to resign, I do not know who actually organized or started the Manila uprising. I do know that General Ramos, who was a close friend and member of the same Protestant church as Salonga, was in command of the armed forces and refused to use them against the nonviolent demonstrators who confronted the tanks and soldiers in the streets.

Salonga had told me on one of my visits to his home that we could not talk in the same room with his telephone, as a military friend had warned him it was wired to pick up any conversation in the room. I knew then that Ramos was protecting him.

Soon after the session at Salonga's home to plan the nonviolent resistance I preached on Sunday, September 16, in Good Samaritan Methodist Church in Quezon City, a part of metropolitan Manila which had more than a million population. That church was the only one in Greater Manila that seemed to take social action and community services seriously. It had a family-planning clinic, a day nursery for the children of working parents, at least one social worker, a nurse, and a physician on its staff. It was located in a poor neighborhood but had a largely middle-class congregation.

After the church service the pastor, Bonifacio Mequi, Jr., introduced me to the editor of *The Manila Times,* José Luno Castro, who invited me to dinner along with Mequi and the head of the National Press Club. From them I learned of the rigid censorship of the press under Marcos. It was not pre-censorship, but immediate review by the President's Public Information staff. Individuals on newspaper staffs who did not conform were dismissed on order of the President, or there were reprisals against the newspaper. These newsmen also told me that as many as three thousand students were involved in the Maoist-led New People's Army, which was operating as an insurrectionary force in Mindinao and also in northern Luzon. These newsmen, who were obviously opposed to martial law, nevertheless felt that it had restored peace in most areas. They reported that various political figures, including some Senators, had their own private armies prior to martial law, that the New People's Army had engaged in violent demonstrations in the streets, and that corruption and bribery was widespread. One of the Union Seminary professors, a Scot, had been shot while driving his Volkswagen through an area frequented by "car-nappers" who stopped cars at machine-gun or rifle point, stole the cars and robbed the occupants.

After our discussion with the newsmen, the pastor drove me to the house of one of his members, Juan Manuel, who was Minister of Education in Marcos' cabinet. Marcos had a number of Protestants or Evangelicals in his cabinet. Some explained this in terms of the President's basic trust in the integrity of Protestants; others pointed out that these people were all relatives of Marcos. General Ramos, head of the Philippine Constabulary and a Protestant, is a cousin of Marcos. Marcos, himself, became a Roman Catholic only when he married at the age of thirty-six. He had been raised in the Acupayan Church, which is related to the Episcopal or Anglican faith tradition.

Secretary Manuel, to my surprise, was a kindly man of about sixty-five who lived in a modest middle class house in an otherwise crowded slum area of Quezon City. We were ushered into a combination dining room-kitchen where we discussed martial law, his philosophy of education, the question of Presidential succession, and other topics. When I reproached him for the compulsory military training (R.O.T.C.) in all the schools, he smiled and said: "It's not our fault. [General Douglas] MacArthur and you Americans fastened that on us."

The next day we set out for Dumaguete, a city of about 50,000. Our family were houseguests of Hubert and Harriet Reynolds, each with a doctorate in anthropology. The tuition at Silliman University, which included schools of law, medicine, theology, engineering, nursing and other subjects, cost at that time a total of $47.00 a semester. The former president of the University had snubbed Marcos when he came to the University in 1972, so Marcos would not permit University fees to be raised and the University radio station had been shut down. Even the newsletter published by the University for students, faculty and alumni had to be sent to Manila for approval by Marcos' staff before it could be published.

While in Dumaguete I visited the provincial jail of Negros Oriental. It was a harrowing experience to see almost three hundred men in an extremely small space. The beds were three decker bunks without any space between them. There were no pads or mattresses on the slats and no windows except at the top on one side. In the tropical heat men got showers only twice a week.

Silliman University was by no means a prison, yet it was surrounded by barbed wire fencing after martial law was declared. There were only a few entrances to the huge campus, where guards carefully checked each person's I.D. card. There was a 10 o'clock curfew, which we violated only for dinner at the President's house.

No one was allowed to enter the grounds of any university in the Philippines without a pass or valid excuse.

My major reason for being in Dumaguete was to speak in the University Lecture Series on American Foreign Policy, but I also addressed classes and professional schools on non-violent change.

After almost a week at Silliman University, we embarked on a freighter for Mindinao, where most of the fighting against Marcos was taking place. Muslims were fighting for a separate identity and an independent government; whereas the New People's Army with units in Mindinao wanted a Maoist-type government. A day and a night later we arrived at Iligan City with about 200,000 population. We were met by a Methodist pastor, Fred Barrera, and driven to Marawi City, a Muslim stronghold in the interior. Since this was not far from the guerrilla fighting, we passed through police or army checkpoints every few miles.

One of my most interesting experiences after our return to Manila was a meeting with some underground leaders. I had been trying to arrange this for months. My wife and I and another couple from the seminary faculty, Dale and Cathy Bruner, were invited to dinner in an affluent section of Manila. Three underground leaders also came to dinner. One of them was a Catholic priest, Edicio de la Torre, then about thirty years of age, intense and charismatic. He was the leader of Christians for National Liberation, but was spending much of his time with the New People's Army. He was also trying to get Muslim insurgents on Mindinao to accept Maoist leadership. For three-and-a-half hours he and I sparred. I asked him if he had abandoned his vocation as a priest. When he said, "No," I asked if killing and recruiting people to kill were a part of his vocation. He indicated that he did not believe he could kill another human being, but he also said that if it were a choice between defending the proletariat and killing a landlord he knew that the landlord should be killed. However, he expected others to do the killing.

De la Torre thought I was unrealistic in urging him to abandon violence and choose a non-violent method of overthrowing the Marcos government. Most of the evening was spent discussing the question of violence versus non-violence. Neither of us, of course, had any idea that Marcos would last another thirteen years as dictator, or that he would be unseated by a massive non-violent uprising of the people of Manila, to which de la Torre would make no contribution, since he was by this time imprisoned. As curfew approached, we drove him through a certain section of Manila, where, at a given point, he asked us to stop. He disappeared into the night, but about a year later was arrested along with twenty-nine others on charges of conspiracy to commit rebellion and with printing, possessing, distributing and circulating subversive materials. In 1986 he was released by Mrs. Aquino after the successful rebellion against Marcos and martial law.

As a part of my educational work I gave a lecture on medical ethics relating to birth control, abortion, artificial insemination, sterilization, and other matters relating to sexual ethics, at the Mary Johnson Hospital, a Protestant institution surrounded by all the pressures of Roman Catholic doctrine and practice. There were thirty medical doctors present, including the hospital's medical director, the chief of family planning and the head of the obstetrics department. There were some trustees of the hospital as well as twenty seminary students and faculty present. An effort had been made to get some Roman Catholic scholars to come to respond, but they did not appear.

The three of us who team-taught a class on Philippine society -- Nathaniel Cortez, Erme Camba, and I -- took our students on field trips. On one occasion we went to the City Hall in Paranaque, a city of about 137,000 people. We talked with city officials and then visited the jail. It was a large room with four cages in it. It was possible to walk around the cages, each of which was about the size of a secretary's desk or a tiger cage in a circus. Three of these were so crowded that the prisoners could not all lie down on the floor at the same time to sleep. There were no beds or bunks. One of the cages had two women and a child of three or four years old in it. I asked the guards if the prisoners had daily work or exercise. They did not. The maximum sentence was one year.

That evening we went with our class to view night life in some Manila suburbs. We saw primitive night clubs with hostesses and a juke box. Most of the hostesses earned their money from drinks and dancing. Some charged 10-15 pesos for spending the night with a customer (one dollar equaled seven pesos). In a swank night club with a 30-piece band we visited a room with a long one-way mirror through which men looked to make their selection of a female companion in the next room. More than a hundred women were lounging in that room. There was air conditioning, unusual for the Philippines, hundreds of customers, and perhaps as many tables. The cost of an overnight companion in that club was 60 to 100 pesos. The poverty of many Filipinos, including college girls who couldn't get jobs to pay their tuition, forced many of the women into this kind of work.

After each field trip we engaged the issues in discussion and analyzed the reasons society acted as it did toward prisoners or women or poverty, as well as the Church's responsibility for social change.

One of the most difficult challenges I faced was getting into one of the concentration camps where Marcos kept his political prisoners. I had been trying to arrange this for weeks without success. On one occasion, Cirilo Rigos took me to one of the camps to make a pastoral call. But even Filipino pastors could not gain admittance except to see one person at the entrance.

The person in charge of all the camps was Brigadier General Ramos, referred to earlier. I had asked Cirilo Rigos, who was Ramos' pastor, if he would make an appointment for me to see the General. On October 12 a message was given to me at the seminary which said, "Appointment with General Ramos is on Wednesday, October 17, at 8:30 a.m. in Camp Crame at his office." I prepared a list of questions in advance because I knew the interview would be brief. One of the questions I asked him was: "What sort of role should the churches play given their tradition of responsible criticism of government?" His brief answer was: "They should support the government and martial law."

When I asked him about the widespread reports of torture in the "detention centers," the official term for concentration camps, Ramos acknowledged that in some cases torture may take place at the time of arrest. But he insisted that there was no torture in any of the camps under his supervision and cited a report of the International Red Cross, whose team had inspected one of the centers. I told him that the National Red Cross organization had served for a long time as a branch of government in many nations to such an extent that no one now believed it was objective. I proposed that he permit Amnesty International to inspect the camps. He said he would not do business with Amnesty International. When

I questioned him further about not permitting an outside investigation, he bristled and said, "We have nothing to hide." At this point I said, "Do you mean, General, that you would let me take a look?" Ramos stared at me for a moment in silence and then said, "Yes." He picked up the telephone and asked a Colonel Resurrección to come up to his office. He instructed the Colonel to let me visit the Camp Crame detention center. The interview was ended, but I was elated at the opportunity.

Colonel Resurrección took me downstairs and assigned a captain in my presence to take me at General Ramos' order to see the detention center. We saw the women's center first, but I became immediately aware that no one wanted to talk to me with the captain present. Therefore, when we approached the large gymnasium in which the men were detained, I said, "Captain, wait here at the door. I am going to look around by myself. If I need you I'll call you." Since he didn't know me but assumed I was important, he obeyed my order. I walked at random between the rows of double-decker bunks and talked to about thirty detainees. I told them I was a member of the national board of the American Civil Liberties Union and would treat anything they said as confidential.

Most of the men were afraid to talk, but a few did discuss conditions under detention. I met lawyers, editors, students, professors, and former public officials who had been rounded up when martial law had been proclaimed over a year earlier. They had been imprisoned for more than a year without charges having been filed against them.

When I returned to the captain, he asked if I wanted to see the detention center at Fort Bonifacio. I told him "Yes," but made an appointment for the following morning. That detention center, which Ramos did not intend that I see, contained a maximum security building which resembled a dungeon -- damp, poorly lighted, and crowded. Most of the prisoners were Maoists, a number of whom were discussing armed revolution during my visit. The minimum security area in another section was clean and free from crowding; it was the most acceptable of the various prisons I saw in the Philippines. In some respects these quarters were better than the Japanese-American concentration camps in the United States which I visited during World War II.

There was a third section I was not permitted to see -- the solitary confinement cells for distinguished opponents of Marcos. Among them were Senators Benigno Aquino and Jose Diokno. Aquino was released years later to go to the United States for medical treatment, with the understanding he would stay in the U.S. When he decided to return, Marcos warned him his life would be in danger. When he did return he was shot, allegedly under orders from Marcos. It is of course Mrs. Aquino who succeeded Marcos as President.

I reported in detail about prison conditions to the non-violent strategy group, but decided to write a report to General Ramos after my return to the U.S. I sent him a two-page evaluation of the detention centers containing twelve points, some favorable, and others not. He never acknowledged my letter. (See my article, "Inside Marcos's Concentration Camps," *Christian Century,* November 13, 1974.)

However, Ramos was not a rigid executor of martial law. At an early meeting I had in Senator Salonga's home, the Senator would not let me talk in the room where the telephone was located. He told me that a general who was a friend of his had warned him that his telephone was "bugged" and would pick up conversation within the room. I assumed the general was Ramos, since they were members of the same church.

On Saturday, October 20, I went at 7 a.m. to the University of the Philippines in Quezon City to lead an hour of Bible study at a student-faculty conference, to be followed by a panel on which I was the moderator. Senator Salonga and others opposed to martial law were on the panel. My Bible study dealt with passages of resistance to government, and with those which are frequently but wrongly interpreted as always requiring support of government as coming from God. After the panel I went with Senator Salonga to his house for lunch and another private discussion of non-violent resistance.

The next day at 7 a.m. a car came from the University, since at 8:30 a.m. I was to preach at a church attended chiefly by government personnel. Then just before 10:00 a.m. we drove to the large University church where I preached to a packed congregation of students and faculty on the text "God has chosen the weak things of the world to confound the things that are mighty."

However, I had heard that Luis Taruc would be at the National Council of Churches building in Manila for an 11 a.m. appointment with me if I could make it. I left the service immediately following my sermon to meet Taruc, who had been the guerrilla leader of the Huks during and following World War II and who after years of imprisonment had been released. He had renounced both the Communism of the Huks and death-dealing violence, and had written a book, *He Who Rides the Tiger,* published in the U.S. by Praeger.

Taruc and I spent three hours discussing non-violent resistance. We went to lunch in a slum district across the street from Knox Church, where I also spoke for two hours on "Liberation in the Bible and Today." Taruc came to the meeting. He was 60 years old then, a Roman Catholic, a widower, with only a high school education. He was now a consultant on land reform to the Secretary of Agriculture, who had insisted on his appointment over the opposition of others in the government. Taruc was no stranger to non-violent action, as he had led a band of peasants to lie down on railroad tracks to stop trains, and had put himself closest to the oncoming train. He had also used non-violent tactics on other occasions during his career. When he came to the U.S. a year later he visited us in Kansas City and spoke at Saint Paul School of Theology.

In the course of teaching and my political activity I was able to conduct several population studies. The chief finding from my research was that in Manila and Cebu, the two largest industrial centers, when large numbers of women worked outside the home, the population rate fell dramatically. Their new source of income and a desire to educate their children led them to use contraceptives. The Philippine population density was greater than that of China, and five times the world average, with more than 290 people per square mile. Although it was essentially an agricultural economy, it could not feed its people with its own rice yield, but was forced to import rice. The daily caloric intake of Filipinos was 35 percent short of the recommended nutritional need of at least 2200 calories per day. The protein shortage was 15 percent less than their needs. Some three million children were suffering from malnutrition, some of them with irreversible brain damage.

A questionnaire which I distributed to medical doctors and to faculty members at several institutions of higher education, included the question: "Who are the chief opponents of birth control?" The results showed, in this order: The Roman Catholic Church, the uneducated, older parents and grandparents, Protestant fundamentalists who misinterpreted Genesis 1:28, and men. The pioneers in birth control were the Mary Johnston Hospital (Methodist) and the National Council of Churches in the Philippines.

However, in 1970 Ruben Tanesco, a Jesuit, told a family planning seminar that "within the whole Catholic Church there are two general views." The first is the view of the Pope and the second is a "dissenting stand." He also said that "the encyclical *Humanae Vitae* is not an infallible document," and "no one will excommunicate you just because you are not following the encyclical." Unfortunately his position was not known in the villages or most urban areas. Even the small Protestant population in the Philippines showed in their own practice the impact of Roman Catholic cultural opposition to birth control. Women were being exploited by "macho" husbands who proved their virility by the number of children they sired. The driver of the Seminary car who drove our family once a week to Manila, had sired twenty-one children and five of his wives had died in the process.

A series of lectures I gave on liberation at the theological school with a large group of others present was evidently reported to the authorities. I learned just before leaving for the U.S. that a military intelligence officer had come to the campus to inquire about an unnamed American who was promoting resistance to martial law and to the government. The first person he interviewed was a professor at Philippine Christian College who had been present at all four lectures. He told the officer that I was a firm believer in nonviolence and that I had opposed violent resistance to the government. The officer was apparently satisfied and left the campus.

At the close of my last public lecture one of my classes presented my wife and me with a beautiful gift of a carved tree stump into which fit wooden pieces that, when all put together, make a large flower growing out of the stump. There were other wood carvings also given to us. We were much moved and were told by another American faculty member that such a presentation was unusual. After that we went to the President's house where the faculty had gathered for its farewell to us. There was a bamboo dance, other music, and a farewell "blessing" speech by President Nacpil, who expressed appreciation for a different and timely approach to ethics given the church-state and violent dimensions of the Philippine situation. They had been for some years surfeited by Bonhoeffer's and Fletcher's "situation ethics," neither of which, he said, dealt adequately with the political situation they faced. (For a discussion of their ethics in contrast to mine, see my book *Liberation Ethics*, Macmillan, 1972.)   During the farewell song our 12-year-old daughter, Joanna, who had not wanted to come to the Philippines but who had grown to love it, could not contain herself and cried. Our son John and younger daughter Jean also found it hard to part from friends made there.

Two busloads of students, the President and all but three of the faculty, drove to the airport to see us off. When we left we realized that this had been our finest overseas experience. The Filipino people are beautiful, industrious, and friendly. I also felt a sense of accomplishment. A regularly meeting group of more than 150 persons was working on non-violent solutions. Senator Salonga and I were to remain in touch for years, though he used assumed names for himself and other persons when he wrote to me. We also remained in touch with Nael Cortez and other faculty and students over the years.

We touched down on Guam and were met in Honolulu, where I spoke at the University of Hawaii on amnesty, on a radio talk show on the same subject, and at various other meetings arranged by the American Friends Service Committee.

Chapter 12
Experience in Africa

Because of my concern for black liberation both in Rhodesia (now Zimbabwe) and South Africa, I went to Africa in 1977 to teach at Epworth Theological College, a black school near Salisbury, Rhodesia. However, I decided to spend part of my sabbatical visiting other countries to learn politically and culturally about the various parts of Africa. My first stop was Addis Abbaba on September 27, where I had only one contact, a Mennonite guest hostel. I soon discovered that Ethiopia was in the throes of a civil war, that there was virtual anarchy in Addis Abbaba, that almost every missionary had left, and that the two Mennonite women who had met my plane were among the few white foreigners still in the country. We drove to the airline office to confirm my next flight. When I got out of the car I was surrounded by about twenty men in their twenties who shouted at me: "You're a missionary here to suck our people's blood." Later, when I walked around the city, there were wandering bands of armed soldiers without an officer and no visible police.

The next day I went to the United Nations headquarters in Africa Hall, a beautiful building on a hill, to talk with Kingsley Dube, Chief of the United Nations Information Service. He described Ethiopia as a "pre-political society with no popular movement, no political consciousness or organization. The Army simply took over and had no respect for the old regime or the church. The result was socialist revolution by edict and decree from above." Mr. Dube gave me a helpful contrast between Soviet and Chinese approaches to Africa, as both groups were present in Ethiopia and in some other countries. The Soviets were attempting to expand their influence and were Ethiopia's principal supplier of arms. "The Chinese have no specific political-military initiatives," he said, "but are building friendship by construction projects, such as building a railroad in Tanzania." Dube gave me my first political and cultural overview of Africa. I left Ethiopia, after several other interviews, for Nairobi on a plane with two Swedes and a number of Chinese workers, one of whom spoke English.

In Nairobi, Melaku Kifle of the Refugee Secretariat of the All-Africa Council of Churches, said there were more than one-and-a-half million refugees from wars, revolutions and dictatorship in Africa. Refugee aid was being coordinated by his Secretariat. Their program of assistance, counseling and placement was the most intelligent and progressive I encountered anywhere in the world.

One of my other interviews in Nairobi was with Simeon Shitemi, Under-Secretary in Kenya's Foreign Ministry in charge of relations with the United States. He told me that if Western powers are not quick enough to be sensitive to change in South Africa, all of southern Africa will be pushed into Marxism. "If Western powers are awake to realities that blacks are determined to be free at all costs, power can be shared among races." He illustrated with Angola and Mozambique, where the U.S. helped the Portuguese try to maintain colonialism. Today, these countries "feel their natural allies are Marxists" because the Russians aided them in their fight against colonialism. He indicated that within the past ten years, American multinational corporations had reaped bigger profits in South Africa than anywhere else in the developing world. "Abandoning support of the [white] South African government may be impossible for the U.S. and Britain, as 67% of business investment in South Africa is British and American."

When I went to South Africa, following visits in rural Kenya, Tanzania, Zambia and Botswana, W.D. Wilson, a top officer in the Anglo-American Corporation, said essentially the same thing: "We face an era of international upheaval and external disapproval. We have too much of what the world wants, so that a boycott is unlikely, but not impossible." He also said, "Change is essential, not merely for profits, but for survival."

In Tanzania, one of my interviews was with Nick Maro, who headed the Ministry of Public Works, Buildings and Transport. He was a graduate of Valparaiso University in Indiana in 1965. He said Tanzania has African socialism, which differs from European varieties. The original conception of socialism was built on African society, where everyone was a worker or farmer. There were no masters, but society owed responsibility to the very young, the disadvantaged and disabled. They were exempted from work, and the government provided for them. "My brother's keeper" is a part of their philosophy. A person with extended family relations has responsibilities to them.

The African tradition, he said, is combined with democracy and the development of a revolutionary party. Since Tanzania was still 96% rural, the major means of production was in the hands of the people. There were constitutional guarantees of freedom of worship and assembly. The law permitted strikes, he said, but they were discouraged.

I also had about an hour with David Mwakawago, the Principal of Kirukani College, which was responsible for ideological and other training of Party leaders and those who went into rural areas to organize the people. There were local councils in villages, urban and rural areas where people discussed the affairs of the country.

In Zambia I talked with Gottfried Geingob, the director of the Namibia Institute, who asserted that when the Southwest Africa People's Organization (SWAPO) takes over Namibia from South Africa, it will be a Marxist state, but conditioned by the local situation. I asked where SWAPO got help. He said, "Western countries refused to give arms to fight white people, so we got them from socialist countries: Russia, China, Cuba and Czechoslovakia. We have had some support from Holland and from private groups in America."

He indicated that the World Council of Churches had given money for medical help and the Lutherans and Anglicans also have helped. He said that because of this help, they had an appreciation for the churches and would guarantee freedom of religion in the new society.

In Zambia I met by chance Daniel Ntoni Nzinga, the General Secretary of the Angola Council of Evangelical Churches. He spoke no English and I no Portuguese, so we conversed in French about the struggle for liberation in Angola, where they were preparing for the first Party Congress. He said that for the first time, as a result of the liberation from the Portuguese, Protestants have the same rights as Roman Catholics and were working out a plan for religious freedom.

I had no difficulty entering South Africa from Botswana, and went immediately to the Johannesburg Friends Meeting House to get an introduction to life in that country. I soon learned that South

Africa is multinational and multi-ethnic, but that one had to seek out the different groups. It was possible to be a tourist in South Africa and never meet black Africans or "Coloured" (persons of mixed race), or Indians, the three groups that were subordinate to white South Africans under apartheid.

In South Africa I went illegally, or without a permit, into Soweto, the revolutionary black center near Johannesburg.   I accompanied a white woman who had a temporary permit.   If caught, my excuse was to be that she needed a male protector; though in fact, she was protecting and guiding me with her many contacts there.   Soweto was, in effect, the black capital of South Africa, and had more professional blacks than elsewhere.   There are also important black areas in Pretoria, Durban, East London, Port Elizabeth, and Capetown.   The size of Soweto was about thirty square miles, with a population of one-and-a-half million. It was the nerve center of Black Africa, as Capetown is for the Coloured, and Durban for Indians.   When I was there, about 10,000 high school students had already begun a militant revolt against the leadership of the adult blacks who had acquiesced in apartheid.

In Johannesburg, I interviewed whites who were thoroughly trusted by blacks.   One of them was Cedric Mayson of the Christian Institute, an interracial organization devoted to non-violent action. He told me that the majority of black ministers in black churches are considered irrelevant; that the problem of the churches, including black ministers, is that they are still trying to talk to Africans about Christianity from a Western point of view.   Mayson said that the youth of Soweto had every one of Martin Luther King's speeches on tape, except for his "I have a dream" speech given at the March on Washington in 1963.   He asked me to get it and send it to him.   The youth of Soweto were pursuing a non-violent strategy at that point.

When I went to Capetown I met and teamed up with a politically sophisticated white woman, a Quaker physician, who took me to the large squatter settlements and introduced me to various black women, and also to black and white leaders in Capetown.   I met Rommel Roberts, a young "Coloured" man, who has organized a non-violent network to warn blacks of police raids.   On other occasions I discussed the use of non-violent strategies with groups of militant black youth, already committed to violent change.

Rommel Roberts told me that government raids on squatter towns and the destruction of their houses had led twenty-one churches to violate the Group Areas Act and the Prevention of Illegal Squatting Act, by erecting tents for squatters on church property. Each of them had between three and fifty-four tents. The government could have prosecuted the ministers, but instead chose to raid the camps. The raids, usually about 3 to 4 a.m., were sadistic, often ending in sexual assaults. The police would also enter the tents, yank the bedclothes off, and watch the women dress. Roberts said that from parked cars near police stations, his group would wait until the police started in the direction of a church, and then notify the church by phone so people could be dressed and out of the tents.

When I went to South Africa I carried press credentials from *The National Catholic Reporter,* whose headquarters is in Kansas City. This obligated me to interview leading Catholic dignitaries as well as other leaders. One of those was Cardinal McCann, Archbishop of Capetown, who illustrated the position of many churches, both Catholic and Protestant. He said: "We have gotten nowhere with our appeals to the government. We have made public declarations and have asked industrialists to help. . . . We can't change the system overnight." I said, "On your desk is the figure of Jesus hanging on the cross. Have you considered the possibility of suffering and imprisonment in this situation?" He responded, "I have allowed squatters to rebuild their houses on church property and stay on church property . . . But the time has not yet come for the kind of action to which you refer."

Before I left South Africa some of the organizations I had visited were raided, and many of the leaders whom I had interviewed were "banned." Cedric Mayson was one of these. I had promised to locate the King tape he requested. I located one in the possession of a Coloured woman in Capetown, made a copy of it, and took it to Johannesburg. Mayson was by this time confined to his home (part of the process of "banning," which also included preventing visitors to him or public declarations by him). I did not want to endanger him, so I found a white woman who was above suspicion to deliver the tape to his wife.

In Rhodesia, now Zimbabwe, I discovered a revolutionary situation. Almost every black family had a son who had joined the "freedom fighters." Many were still in their teens, and affectionately called "the boys." I taught in a black college; lived alone in a cottage on the edge of the campus about seventeen miles from Salisbury, which I was told was sometimes frequented by guerrillas ("the boys") at night. The freedom fighters were everywhere; they controlled some of the countryside during the day and much of it at night. None of the major roads could be traveled at night and even in daylight some could be traveled only once or twice a day in armed convoys.

The white government had moved hundreds of thousands of Africans into "Protected Villages" ("P.V.s") in order to deny "terrorists" (the freedom fighters, or "the boys") access to them. I was able to persuade the government ministry in charge to let me visit one. A public relations officer drove me 200 miles to see one good enough to show a foreign visitor. The last stretch of the journey had just been cleared of land mines before we arrived. About 1,700 people lived inside a high fence in a collection of round huts, guarded by black soldiers with white officers. During the day the people could leave to walk five to ten miles to allotted plots of ground where they were permitted to have a garden. They could not carry any food with them, and had to return before curfew, or sleep on the ground outside the fence.

Several years before I left for Africa, I had met the Methodist bishop of Rhodesia, Abel Muzorewa. He had been speaking in the United States on non-violent resistance to the white Rhodesian government, but subsequently had changed his mind about violence. I had debated him before about six hundred people at a California summer conference (Asilomar), on the issue of violence and revolution in a strongly-worded session. Nevertheless, when I called on him in Salisbury, he offered to put his office and car at my disposal. One day I had lunch with him in his house, surrounded by a high steel wall and armed guards. I tried again to persuade him to become a non-violent leader, but without success.

Muzorewa, who had no experience in office outside the church, but intended to run for the office of Prime Minister when the country achieved independence from Britain, asked me many questions that day about how to run a government, as he knew I had a doctorate in political science. One of the questions I recall was what position to take on capital punishment. When our visit was over, his chauffeur and another armed guard drove us to his next appointment and to mine. I saw him on several other occasions, and even conspired to change his mind. I worked out a total and detailed program for nonviolent overthrow of the Ian Smith government and arranged a meeting with the leaders of his Women's Political Party. After several hours of discussion, they agreed to the general outline of the program, including a nationwide boycott, and set a date to discuss it with him one morning. It was obvious to them and to me that Muzorewa had not captured the mind and mood of the people, as Nkomo and Mugabe were doing in their guerrilla leadership. It was not because they were violent, but because Muzurewa was doing nothing in the way of resistance.

I made an appointment with him at 2 p.m. the same day as the Women's group had met with him. I outlined again some essential strategies of resistance. He didn't realize there had been any collusion, and expressed astonishment that his women's group had come to a similar conclusion. He rejected the proposal as entailing too much danger to him and the black population. It was at that point I urged him not to run for office. Again he told me what he said in my earliest interview with him: "I am not really interested in being in government or in politics. I came because I was asked by the people to lead . . . If people of this country elected another leader, I would feel free to step down."

After I had returned to the States, I had a letter from his secretary asking me to provide him information on how to conduct a political campaign, raise funds, etc. I wrote him a detailed response. He did become Prime Minister in what was to be a transition government, and collaborated with the Ian Smith political forces, to his detriment. After that he lost all political influence, but was unwilling to leave politics.

One of the creative forces in Rhodesia was the Catholic Peace and Justice Commission, a mixed racial group which had taken on the enormous job of documenting cases of torture and brutality by the white government of Ian Smith. The Commission office and the homes of its officers were raided, files were confiscated, and the officers arrested. At their request I met with the full Commission for their first full discussion of the philosophy and techniques of non-violent action. The meeting, scheduled for an hour, lasted three, and led to subsequent discussions with their officers.

At Epworth Theological College I tried to make three contributions. One was a theology of liberation, which was well-received. My second emphasis on non-violence fell on ears of those already convinced that freedom depended on guerrilla war. The third was a discussion of Marxism and the outline of the Christian-Communist dialogue that had taken place in France, Czechoslovakia and the United States in the years just preceding.

On one occasion, when Mrs. Verna Culver, who taught the wives of the African ministerial students, was away for several days, I had the opportunity for a totally female class discussion. The place of women in that society was one greatly subordinate to men. It was the custom of women approaching a black leader such as a bishop, to fall on their knees and approach him on their knees. In that class I asked what they as women could do to help liberate their country. They were unanimous in saying that "the boys" would do the liberating. We talked about cooperative agricultural work, sharing produce, buying clubs, and a boycott of industrial and imported goods, among other ways they could share in the task of liberation.

One of my memorable trips inside Rhodesia was across the country to Old Umtali Mission in the east, where our convoy had to arrive before curfew. There, instead of making my own meals in my cottage, I ate African fare as the poorest of Africans did, saw a model African farm, and observed the largest private school in Rhodesia in session. Another memorable trip was with Dean Culver and his wife Verna to the famous Zimbabwe ruins, easily one of the seven or ten wonders of the world, and the next day to a large animal preserve to see all varieties of African animals in the wild. We had the experience there of a lion jumping on the hood of our parked car.

My visits to South Africa and Rhodesia were in a real sense the climax of my trip to Africa. The ending of government by whites only when Rhodesia became Zimbabwe was an achievement that would only be surpassed when South Africa became a democracy rather than a minority white government. I left Rhodesia by flying to Johannesburg. On my way north from South Africa I visited Gabon; stayed in the Cameroons with Steane Eko, an African student of mine when we were both in the Philippines; and was the guest, at the University of Lagos and the University of Ibadan in Nigeria, of the Vice-Chancellor of each of those great universities, where I was scheduled to deliver lectures.

The living conditions for most urban dwellers in the Cameroons and the big cities in Nigeria are unbelievably bad. The climate is steaming hot and the housing poor and crowded. I slept two nights in the bed of my former student in an inside room with no window or ventilation and no water, in great heat, before acknowledging to myself that I couldn't take it. Such heat and housing conditions inevitably mean that millions of West Africans are out in the streets until late at night.

In Nigeria I had excellent interviews and learned much about the culture of West Africa. The most exciting event there occurred when Nigerian Airways, without notice, cancelled my flight from Ibadan to Lagos. I teamed up with a Nigerian, hired a taxi for $40, and bribed and persuaded the police at three checkpoints, to get to Lagos by the next morning. Only cars holding special passes were permitted to travel the expressway. I had to go through passport control three times, and currency control twice, and talk my way on to the plane to Douala in the Cameroons, as the plane had been oversold and my name had been omitted from the list.

My last stop in Africa was in Liberia. I was met at the airport by Charles Nance, the administrative assistant to the Vice President of Liberia, Bennie Warner, who was also the Methodist bishop, and driven forty-two miles to Monrovia, the capital. President William L. Tolbert, Jr., who was also for some years a President of the World Baptist Alliance, had asked Bishop Warner only about a month previously to be his Vice-President, chiefly because of the moral leadership he had given to the nation in eradicating corruption and the abuse of power in the country. Warner also had good relations with Muslims and with Roman Catholic and Lutheran leaders. It was obvious that Liberia did not have separation of church and state, although in many respects it was patterned after the U.S. government. Warner told me that every church has private schools and that the government provided a 25% to 50% subsidy to the church schools.

Warner also spoke of the tremendous problems of Liberia, a nation with 80% illiteracy, large-scale unemployment, and a need for educational and health facilities. One of the persons I interviewed was Frances Caulker, the education officer of the Family Planning

Association of Liberia. She said that Liberia had a 3.3% rate of population growth, among the highest in the world, and that for every four women between the ages of 14 and 45, three were pregnant at any one moment. The 1974 census reported that the average number of children born to each woman was 6.0, and the number surviving was 3.0. In the ten-year period 1965-1975, Liberia had the largest absolute increase in birth rate of any country in the world, increasing from 43 per 1000 to 50 per 1000. Yet the government had no declared population policy other than certain privileges given to the Family Planning Association such as rent-free headquarters, a duty-free privilege of importing contraceptives, a free utility service and a $5,000 subsidy toward the F.P.A. budget.

When I left Africa to return to the United States I was very much aware that I had received a far greater education about Africa than anything I was able to give to my students. In retrospect, the knowledge gained of the South African scene was invaluable, and worth the whole trip. One of my many unreported interviews was with Alan Boesak, a "Coloured" Dutch Reformed minister in South Africa, who had just written *Farewell to Innocence,* a survey of black theologies of liberation. He was an admirer of Martin Luther King, at least tentatively committed to nonviolent action, and was on his way to becoming the best-known church spokesman for liberation other than Bishop Desmond Tutu. His courage and leadership I found equaled or nearly equaled by numerous other men and women who are building the new Africa from the ashes of white Western colonialism.

Chapter 13
The American
Committee on Korea

In 1993 there was a belligerent tone in the press about the possibility of war between the U.S. and Korea. Some politicians and columnists were accusing North Korea of developing nuclear weapons. I had no special interest in Korea, though I had written a chapter about the U.S. and Korea in my 1970 book, *American Empire*.

However, I was invited to speak to the 27th Annual Conference of the Association of Korean Christian Scholars in North America in July 1993. A few weeks after that I was invited to speak to an International Conference of Koreans in September in Los Angeles. They came from Japan, South Korea, Canada, and the U.S. Preparation for these events and discussions with several Korean leaders led me to ask whether they would welcome the formation of an American Committee on Korea to try to prevent the war being discussed in the press. They liked the idea.

Later that year I formulated the following as the purposes of that Committee:

1. To inform and arouse the conscience of Americans about the U.S. occupation of Korea and its continuing military and economic actions therein.

2. To ask the U.S. government to conclude a peace treaty with North Korea, ending the Korean War that was merely suspended in 1953.

3. To work for the withdrawal of American troops and weapons from Korea.

4. To work for a denuclearized and disarmed Korea.

5. To work for the reconciliation and unification of North and South Korea.

In forming the Committee I asked Catholic, Jewish, Protestant and secular leaders whom I had known for years and who have a concern for peace and disarmament and who also oppose imperialism. Only two of the number I asked turned me down. Five of those invited I did not know personally. Within three weeks we had a committee of 38 well-known leaders.

We produced and distributed thousands of leaflets alerting peace and religious organizations to the danger of war and on numerous occasions I spoke to groups across the country.

When I went to North Korea in May 1994 the newspapers in the United States were depicting that country as a Stalinist dictatorship preparing nuclear weapons and threatening war. Secretary of Defense William Perry was talking about a possible "pre-emptive strike" on the North Korean nuclear reactor. In short, the process of demonizing North Korea was well under way (as Vietnam, Panama, and Iraq had been demonized before we went to war with them).

Two Korean Americans who accompanied us had been there before and were fluent in the Korean language, Dr. Harold Sunoo and Rev. Kilsang Yoon. It was necessary for us to go first to Beijing, since the United States does not permit direct travel to North Korea. The U.S., never willing to end the Korean war of 1950-53 with a peace treaty and diplomatic recognition, has isolated that country with an economic embargo and would not even permit phone calls from the U.S. to North Korea.

The North Koreans, not surprisingly, had quite human faces and treated us with friendship and government hospitality. They had no restrictions on phone calls; each of us was able to phone our respective homes in the United States. They planned to show us their most important tourist spots, but after two days of such tours they readily permitted us to determine our own itinerary.

Most important on any list of things to see was the huge concrete wall initiated by the U.S. military and built by South Korean soldiers and workers entirely across the nearly 150-mile-wide peninsula. A demarcation line costing hundreds of millions of dollars, the wall is 16 to 26 feet high and from 9 to 22 feet in width at the top, with a base 32 to 60 feet wide. It is the most visible symbol of the Cold War, far greater than the 27-mile Berlin Wall.

One difference between the Berlin Wall, built by European communists, and the wall built by South Korea, was "Checkpoint

Charlie," which permitted Germans and tourists to cross through the wall for visits. In Korea the U.S. and South Korean military do not permit visits by any of the approximately ten million divided family members, some of them refugees in the South from the Korean war. A former president or an important U.S. official can be let through, but no regular visits are possible.

Our most important discussions were with Kim Yong Sun, the Secretary of the Central Committee of the Workers Party of Korea, who is in a key position in charge of major committees, including the Anti-Nuclear Peace Committee. In our first three-hour session he wanted to know about the American Committee on Korea and to test my knowledge or expertise on U.S. foreign and military policy. Then he presided at a banquet for us and some of his deputies. It was a formal occasion where I responded to his toast and he talked to us about his work.

On a second occasion we had a several-hour session in which we discussed a range of North Korean policies on foreign relations, the economy, nuclear weapons, and reunification. Again he expressed his appreciation to us with a formal banquet.

In those discussions I made a series of proposals that I believed would ease tensions with the United States and lead to better relations. These were essentially the same that former President Jimmy Carter made a few weeks later when he met with Kim Yong Sun and Kim Il Sung. It was Carter's prestige and skill that changed the climate in the U.S. and North Korea from one of war to one of peace. We had no contact with Carter until after he returned to the U.S.

After visiting North Korea we went to Japan and met leaders of the Korean community in Tokyo. I had a half-hour meeting with U.S. Ambassador Walter Mondale, to whom I reported my discussions and impressions while in North Korea.

Thereafter, I spent a week in South Korea speaking, holding press conferences, and meeting with U.S. Ambassador James Laney and some church and government leaders in Seoul.

When I preached in one of the Methodist churches in Seoul, a coincidence that is hard to believe occurred. One of those in attendance was Edicio de la Torre, a Catholic priest and an underground leader of the violent resistance to the Marcos dictatorship while I was in the Philippines during my sabbatical there in 1973. In a meeting dangerous to him since he had a price on his head, we had argued violence and nonviolence as the way to oppose Marcos. I did not recognize him when he introduced himself after the church service in Seoul. He said he had left the priesthood, and acknowledged that I was right in preparing the way for non-violent resistance.

South Korea was no democracy. The Korean CIA prohibited the newspapers, radio, and TV from reporting my press conferences and other activities there, although the North Korean press had done so while I was in the North. Moreover, almost half of the people at my final meeting in Seoul, including church, labor, and university personnel, had been arrested or imprisoned by the government for nonviolent activities such as speaking or organizing.

Space does not permit further observations about Korea or my subsequent trip to North Korea in 1995. However, upon my return to the U.S. in 1994 I spoke again to an International Conference of Koreans that met at the University of Maryland, and have on various occasions met with the North Korean ambassador to the United Nations, the State Department Chief of Intelligence on Korea, and the Assistant Secretary for Human Rights, as well as concerned Korean Americans.

Although talk of war has receded and relations with Korea have improved, I have continued my non-salaried position as executive secretary of the American Committee on Korea, but with far less activity than in 1994 and 1995.

Chapter 14
Conclusion

Over a period of thirty-six years in seventy-nine different countries, in some cases for extended visits, I became more firmly convinced that human rights, religious liberty, and political freedom are intertwined. Each of the three is dependent on the other two.

Even where there is political freedom and national religious liberty, a powerful international organization can exercise dominion over some or all of its members, as Hans Küng, the eminent Catholic theologian, reminded us in 1985 when he wrote: "No one is burned at the stake anymore, but careers and psyches are destroyed as required." People are still attacked for their lack of religious conformity or orthodoxy. Some are shot and killed by religious zealots, and there are still basically religious wars in parts of the world.

It is essential to remember that throughout history there have been religious wars as well as political and civil wars. Both the state and organized religion have at times been tyrannical. Religious persecution has been almost as frequent as political repression. Even today religious and political liberty do not exist in many nations. And generally where one exists, the other also does.

The surest guarantee of religious liberty in any nation is separation of church and state. A state-established religion or one that is state-financed or endorsed is not free. Separation is essential to permit voluntarism to flourish and to prevent discrimination on the basis of religion.

The following reasons summarize why separation is essential for both religious groups and the state:

- It prevents the state from claiming divine approval and hence claiming it is above criticism.
- Separation prevents the government from determining either directly or indirectly the policy of religious organizations.

- Separation does not permit religious organizations to seek special privileges from government that are denied to minority religious groups and to those who are religiously unaffiliated.
- Religious organizations are healthier and stronger if they must assume responsibility both for financing their own programs and for stimulating their members to accept that responsibility.
- By operating independently of government aid, churches, mosques and synagogues deny to government the power to impose compulsory tithes on all taxpayers, believers and non-believers alike. They thus avoid the resentment of those who do not want to be forced to contribute to that to which they do not belong and of their own members who do not welcome being forced to contribute through government action.
- Since separation precludes financial support or special privilege from government, religious groups are free to engage in prophetic criticism of the government and to work for social justice.
- The mission of churches is compromised by government aid to church schools that serve chiefly middle and upper class students. Church empires are costly and require additional private funds from those who use the services, thus tending to exclude millions of poor people.
- Government sponsorship of religious activity, including prayer services, sacred symbols, religious festivals, holidays and the like, tends to secularize the religious activity rather than make government more ethical or religious.
- Finally, the witness of religious groups is greater in any nation if they are not identified with or dependent upon specific governments. The Reformed Church was for years identified with the old all-white government of South Africa. The Roman Catholic Church was closely identified with the Franco and Salazar dictatorships in Spain and Portugal. More recently, the Serbian Orthodox Church has been identified with the policies of Serbia, the Roman Catholic Church with Croatia and Islam with Bosnia.
- It is also possible that government aid to a particular religion may take sides in an intra-organizational controversy, as has occurred within a church where numerous parents do not want religious education concentrated in a system of parochial schools

but want it available also to their children who attend public schools. Or as one parish put it, "We voted in our parish not to have a parish school and we certainly do not want the state to make us pay taxes to support other church schools."

When the United States was formed as a republic and the Constitution was adopted, separation of church and state, separation of powers (executive, legislative, and judicial) and federalism were incorporated as principles of the new nation, although none was identified by the above titles. Article VI, Section 3 provided for separation of church and state. It requires all "officers both of the United States and of the several states . . . to support this constitution but no religious test shall ever be required as a qualification to any office or public trust under the United States."

This was followed by the First Amendment, which says, "Congress shall make no law respecting an establishment of religion or prohibiting the free exercise thereof."

An "establishment of religion" had two meanings then, as it does now. An establishment is an institution. Establishment also means a religious institution sponsored or supported by the government.

At the time the First Amendment was adopted, six states had multiple establishments of religion, or aid provided to all churches in each state on a non-preferential basis. It was this practice that the amendment forbade Congress to adopt. It did not refer to a single national church, as in England, where the Anglican Church was and is the established church. Most people in the United States in 1791 had lived in America for generations under American-type establishments, or free churches outside government establishment.

Official separation of church and state has meant a secular Constitution which neither aids or inhibits religion.

When that principle is threatened either by the state or religious groups, the liberty of all is under attack.

About the Author

John Swomley holds a doctorate in political science from the University of Colorado and is an ordained United Methodist minister. From 1960 to 1984 he was Professor of Christian Ethics at the St. Paul School of Theology in Kansas City. He served as executive secretary of the Fellowship of Reconciliation from 1953 to 1960 and of the National Council Against Conscription from 1944 to 1952.

He is president of Americans for Religious Liberty and served for many years on the national board of the American Civil Liberties Union. He also served on the Board of Consultants of the Midwest Bioethics Center, is currently on the advisory board of Planned Parenthood of Greater Kansas City and has been active in the Religious Coalition for Reproductive Choice.

His articles have appeared in *Christian Social Action, The Christian Century, The National Catholic Reporter, USA Today, The Nation, The Saint Louis Journalism Review, The Humanist, The Saint Louis University Public Law Review,* and *The Churchman/Human Quest.*

His published books include *The Military Establishment; American Empire; Liberation Ethics; The Politics of Liberation; Religion, the State, and the Schools; Religious Liberty and the Secular State; Myths About Public School Prayer; Religious Political Parties; Abortion and Public Policy.*